A Remembrance

By Brett Connell

ISBN 978-0-9974541-1-6

Contact the Author:
Brett Connell
shiningyourglory@gmx.com

Special thanks to: Jesus Christ, Nancy Connell, Evangelist Barbara Lynch, Reverend Christopher Gore, Duncan & Lynda Connell. Thank you so much for all the support, encouragement and help in making this book possible.

Table of Contents

Chapter 1: The Love of God

Chapter 2: The Journey Into Darkness

Chapter 3: The Dreams

Chapter 4: Being Born Again

Chapter 5: The First Assignment

Chapter 6: The Second Assignment

Chapter 7: Words of Wisdom

Chapter 8: The Third Assignment

Chapter 9: America

Chapter 10: The End Times

Chapter 11: The Death of the Flesh

Chapter 12: Spiritual Warfare

Chapter 13: The Church

Chapter 14: The Legal System

Chapter 1: The Love of God

Do you believe in the love of God? That is a question that will take time for you to answer. But as for me, I can already answer that. I have already gone through many grueling years and have experienced many things to be able to draw my conclusion. I do believe in the love of God, wholeheartedly. I will walk you through the milestones in my life, to which you can personally relate to. You will see as you walk with me the dire situations I faced and how the love of God spared me from certain failure. As you read and understand the daily challenges I faced, that we all face, and see God's Hand intervene in my life you will be inclined to agree that there was a supernatural force at work.

One of the greatest signs that God's love can change people forever is by how other people have reacted to the change in their lives. Over the years, I have been reshaped and reformed. My attitudes, personality, outlooks and lifestyle have changed dramatically. For me personally, I didn't find this through medication or prescriptions, nor through psychiatrists or self-help sessions. I was changed by nothing more than dreams and visions and the voice of God in my spirit. This great reshaping has been the best experience of my life, but it has also come at a cost. I have lost many friends, some of which I had been good friends with for over a decade. They knew the 'old' me, and they were used to me being a certain way. They could not accept the 'new' me that I was becoming, even if it was a better 'me'. It was the simple act of changing they could not tolerate, whether it was for better or worse. This opened my eyes to understand the nature of the human heart.

There are many people who have difficulty accepting change. This is because people become conditioned to their surroundings and circumstances. When your brain is exposed to a repetitive pattern or habit, it grows accustom to that behavior. Changing these established orders and routines takes time, and requires lots of effort.

As God changed me, there were people around me that did not understand and could not adapt to the changes that were taking place in me. I felt guilty as I was being separated from my friends, but I am glad that God did not allow that to stop me from growing.

It truly takes the Spirit of God to lead, guide and direct us into this change of heart. But this can only happen if our hearts are truly open and willing, with enough sense to understand why these changes are taking place and to see the positive benefit of them.

The heart is very important; it is the root of our ability to serve God. At one point in my walk with

God, a relative of mine was going through a season of trials. The enemy, who is the devil, threw very powerful fiery darts at them, and as I watched them going through such challenging circumstances, I began to pray for them. In my prayer, I asked the Lord to show them more grace and favor. I pleaded with the Lord, saying, "Lord, look how hard they work every day and how they try their best to support their family even with hindering circumstances. Then look upon me, someone who does very little in the world, and yet you have shown me such great grace. Why will you not shower the grace upon them that you have showered upon me?" The Lord soon after spoke to me replying, "It does not matter how hard you work or what you do. What matters is an open heart that is obedient." What God was saying to me is essentially Isaiah 64:6 (NIV) "All of us have become like one who is unclean, and all our righteous acts are like filthy rags; we all shrivel up like a leaf, and like the wind our sins sweep us away." But God's grace is the only thing that gives us what we have; we cannot earn it or deserve it, no matter what we do or how hard we try.

Having an open heart to listen for the voice of God, and having the faith and will to obey that voice at all cost – is how you truly serve God. Our Father delights when we praise and worship Him. He knows that even our best works are still as filthy rags. We can never meet His standard of Holiness for living our lives, but through faith in Christ we can be made righteous by His blood and presented to our Father as Holy. You have been purchased by God for a very heavy price, so how will you repay your Father in Heaven? You should do so by becoming obedient to God and doing His will over yours, and allowing Him to reshape and form you to be as He created you to be.

God will not go against your will, either. You have free will, a gift from God. It is up to you whether you choose to serve Him or not. Many people have the misconception that they can dictate how they serve God, and still be alright. Many people believe that by praising and worshiping, and attending services each week that they are saved. This is far from the truth, because your salvation is a daily struggle. The enemy is strong and powerful, ruthless and cunning. He knows that you can serve God all your life, yet if you were to die in unrepentant sin, he would eternally steal you away from God.

Revelation 3:5 (NIV) says, “The one who is victorious will, like them, be dressed in white. I will never blot out the name of that person from the book of life, but will acknowledge that name before my Father and his angels.” This means that the righteous who work out their salvation daily will win the reward, but those who live in unrepentant sin, who are deceived into believing they are saved when they are not; face the possibility of having their names blotted out of the book of life.

Saints, your salvation must be worked out each day as you serve The Lord. Do not underestimate what Jesus did for you, and do not take lightly the battleground you surely walk upon. The war has been won already, but we must still fight daily for the Kingdom of God. If your weapon becomes dull, and your armor weakened, you will surely be overcome and destroyed. Tune and polish your armor daily, sharpen your sword daily, and go forth each day living in the Word of God and following Christ with all your heart with total obedience. God may call you, but will He choose you also? Matthew 22:14 (NLT) says “For many are called, but few are chosen.” How do you know what calling you have on your life? How do you know the depth of that calling? Do you know truly why you are here?

As you walk with God, you will begin to understand more about His timing. The most difficult transition is learning to let go of your own expectation of things, and to surrender your own time table and allow God to work His perfect plan for your life. There have been countless times I have wanted something right then and there, but was not allowed to have it. I became impatient, angry, and upset at God. But as I waited, things unfolded and became clearer through time and circumstances –

and I began to see, in this case, the reasons why I needed to wait. As humans with limited capacity, we cannot see the ditches that have been dug by the enemy for us to fall into. But trusting God that He knows all and sees all, will make our path straight and narrow assuring we will stay on solid ground.

One such thing we learn about timing is when our true calling is revealed to us. God brings forth His will at the right time, every time. I was introduced to Christ at 13 years of age, but I was not saved and didn't truly understand Christ until I was in my late-20's, and from there I did not understand what God's purpose was for my life until I was 27 years old. The only reason I was able to hear the calling of God was because my heart was being worked on for decades to be open and receiving enough to hear the voice of God. I had to be raked over the coals and put through the furnace of affliction to burn away the impurities of my heart before I surrendered to God. Only then, will you hear His voice and know the calling He has placed on your life. God will never go against your will; if you choose to harden your heart and not surrender to God, He will never be able to use you for the greater works of the Kingdom in which you have an inheritance.

As humans, we often want instant gratification. We desire to see instant results, and we also want to see the fruits of our labor. Many people start serving God with enthusiasm and vigor, with the expectation of receiving gifts, blessings, riches or otherwise. After all, God is loving and giving and desires to bless us, right? While those attributes do apply to God and are accurate, serving God is more than give-and-take. 1 Corinthians 6:20 (NIV) says, “you were bought at a price. Therefore honor God with your body.” God paid the ultimate price for you, He gave His one and only son Jesus Christ to die in your place for your sins, and redeem you unto the Father in Heaven. God owes you absolutely nothing, and we owe Him absolutely everything. Yet He still showers us with gifts when we don't deserve it, and could never earn it. Let everything you do be for the Glory of God, and serve Him out of thankfulness in your heart and not out of expectation.

It is not possible for us to fully understand God or His ways, but we can spend our lifetime learning about Him and getting closer to Him. We may come to an understanding of what Christ did for us on the cross, but we may not fully understand the Word of God. I found myself in a situation such as this, and came to the understanding that there is more to the bible than just the gospel. Matthew 5:18 (NIV) says, “For truly I tell you, until heaven and earth disappear, not the smallest letter, not the least stroke of a pen, will by any means disappear from the Law until everything is accomplished.” The law is the spoken Word of God, and everything that is in the word. Therefore every letter of it that applied then is still true today. Jesus says in Matthew 5:17

(NIV) "Do not think that I have come to abolish the Law or the Prophets; I have not come to abolish them but to fulfill them."

In the final age, we will know and understand God completely. But as we are here to do the works for the Kingdom of Heaven, knowing our Father as best we can will aid us in the mission we agreed upon and volunteered for before the foundation of this world.

I know with every fiber of my being that I am a spirit that is temporarily housed within a fleshly container. I know I was created in the image of God, before the foundation of this world. I know that I existed in Heaven, in the presence of our Lord and God. In my great joy, my overwhelming love for my Father, I excitedly and boldly offered to be a part of His plan and will. I knew my Father was perfect, righteous and justified in all His ways – I simply couldn't sit still in all His Glory and Holiness! I asked to be born, and I volunteered for the plan He would make for my life on Earth. I received instruction, and warning, and departed into the womb. Being in the flesh hindered my spirit, and being born into the sin of the world separated me from God, but His Holy Spirit was always upon me. At God's timing, the Holy Spirit urged me and nudged me into position and taught me all over again how to seek the voice of my King and God. Being reborn through Christ, I arose from the ashes of the world and sin, and came to know my Father more clearly and get back into the place I was once in. It took me many years to "get back to my spiritual senses" but now I have a better understanding of what life is really about.

The meaning of life is this: To love and serve God. We can all come up with an idea of how we desire to serve God, in our own time or in our own way. While it is true that God made us all unique with personalities to be used in different ways for His purposes, we must remember that it is His purpose altogether. If everything we do is for the glory of God, then first we must listen for His instruction on what to do. The truth is God doesn't owe us anything. We deserve death and eternal separation. But by the Grace of God, we are redeemed in Christ and we are able to be used by God. We are not the ones who choose the when and the how – we must listen to God with an open heart and obedience. Our own labor will be fruitless in the Kingdom of God, but by His leading and following His Will, He will bless our hands and the fruits of our labor – for our good and His Glory.

Chapter 2: The Journey Into Darkness

There is a saying that goes, "The Will of God will never take you where the Grace of God cannot keep you." and in my experience I have found that to be true, and the Scripture that reflects a similar truth is that of 1 Corinthians 10:13 (NIV) which says, "No temptation has seized you except that which is common to man. And God is faithful; He will not let you be tempted beyond what you can bear. But when you are tempted, He will also provide a way out so that you can stand up under it."

In my youth, I was not very close to God and I never went to church as I was growing up. I never learned or understood the importance of Jesus Christ or who He was. There were many things that happened in my early years that I did not understand, and many other things that were not explained to me. Unbeknown to me at the time, there was a very high and deep calling on my life from Almighty God. This attracted the attention of the enemy, Satan. The truth was, I was under spiritual and demonic attack. Without hesitation, Satan threw everything he had at me since I was in the womb. Every trap was set, every weapon in his arsenal was used to take me down and knock me out, keeping me as far away from God as possible.

I had little knowledge of the Word of God, and little encouragement from peers to explore the bible. In all truth, we had a stable family and bibles in our home; I just never had the wisdom to use it as a resource to help with my problems. I took every spiritual and demonic attack as though it were fleshly and personal. Let me elaborate on this; a spiritual and demonic attack can come in the form of darkness (evil intentions) inside of a person coming against the light in you. Demons influence and persuade the behavior of others to come against you, simply because the darkness in them cannot stand the presence of Christ in you, nor the destiny God has given you. In my lack of knowledge and wisdom, I grew very bitter and angry towards humanity. I had assumed it was only people being mean towards me for no reason. I felt so tormented and neglected by people; I gravitated towards the dark side because I held on to sins of bitterness, unforgiveness, anger and rage.

By the time I was 13 years old, I had already sold my soul to satan in exchange for black magic and power. I had learned to cast curses on people and made my enemies break their bones and become very ill. These things I picked up from classmates in my school and it came to me pretty easily. I succumbed to these things mainly because the weakest area of my life was being vulnerable and not accepted. Satan promised me acceptance and great power, and as I walked through his kingdom and used his power I began to see the effects of what I was doing. This was rooting and grounding myself deeper in his dark territory. I partook in blood covenants, animal sacrifices, rituals, and many other abominable things against humanity, and against the Spirit of God. I committed horrible acts against others, and the demonic influence I allowed inside of me gave me very detailed and powerful instructions on how to do things to please myself and never get caught – and I never did. They would offer ideas, impulses, and introduce thoughts to me. It was my own will and choice to entertain those thoughts and feelings. By opening the door for them, I allowed them to work in me and through me.

The kingdom of darkness worked through me in a very acute way. I would have sudden urges to bring these morbid and twisted ideas into reality. I would suddenly have a strategy and plan, every detail laid out before me and every contingency worked out. When I served the devil, I premeditated everything. I was empowered with great demonic wisdom and intellect. I had every detail planned out and every strategy refined perfectly. My work was very dexterous, very meticulous. I was a perfectionist when it came to getting what I wanted, and I got it every time. I even had demonic influence and the persuasive power of the prince of this world. I swam in an ocean of perversion; I had lost my sense of morality and conscience. The only thing I lived for was doing as much as I possibly could for myself – because everything I wanted for myself I could get, and the feeling of unlimited power was the stronghold that held me in place to continue my sin.

Just like the enemy, who can appear as an angel of light – deception was the greatest tool in my arsenal. There were always running jokes, and fleeting suspicions about my intentions and demeanor. People joked about me being messed up, but none of them ever knew the depth of my servitude to Satan. I was quiet, funny, and very calculating. I was engrossed in the pleasure of being able to manipulate and control the circumstances, and how people around me perceived me. I reveled in the demonic wisdom that was bestowed upon me to accomplish such things, yet in my arrogance I believed that it was my own intellect and power. I became so cocky about myself and boasted of my intellectual pride. But I made sure never to be abrasive to those around me – because I always kept my options open for using them.

I spent much of my time alone and isolated. I enjoyed the darkness and the night, and I always slept during the day. Many times I would find myself just talking to no one in the room – having a full conversation with myself, talking about making plans and strategies to get what I wanted. I felt like a forensics expert that knew every slight detail that everyone else would overlook. As I talked out loudly to an empty room, I would suddenly receive answers and ideas to my topics. What was happening was the demonic realm within me and around me was also having conversations with me. They were talking to me, teaching me, and leading me to do the dark things I desired to further their kingdom.

The enemy had me working for him for many years of my life, and I was happy in it. But this is where the journey began to take a turn, because Almighty God had different plans for my life.

Chapter 3: The Dreams

As I was growing up, I always had a sense of God in the back of my mind. But I never really understood God or what He was all about. I could read the bible and learn values, lessons and principles but could never absorb them into my spirit. I was so bound up with demons, not even one seed of the Word could take root within me. At the time, I wasn't aware of these facts. I was literally blinded and aimless in my half-hearted walk with God. The transition was slow, and very subtle. But it was brought about by things happening to me that I could not explain.

I began to have dreams at night, strange occurrences and happenings that grabbed my attention. One night, I had a dream that was rather bizarre. My driveway became a gathering for an audience of people. There was a wrestling ring at the center of my driveway, and the wrestlers were coming towards the ring in large trucks with lift kits and unrealistically large tires. As the wrestlers got into the ring, and the crowd was cheering, I remember looking at the trucks leaving my driveway. They were driving erratically and swerving away, and one of them clipped a tree at the end of the driveway and it fell down into the road. When I went down there to look at the tree, it was moved from the road back into my property in a certain position that I remembered clearly.

After this, I woke up and thought it was strange but shrugged it off. As I proceeded with my regular late afternoon routine of getting dressed and ready, I went into the kitchen to make a pot of coffee. As I was walking around the kitchen, I peered out the dining room window and saw a sight that froze me in my tracks. I saw the very same tree, in the exact same position as in my dream. I asked my mother what happened to that tree, and she said earlier this morning it had fallen and gone into the road. Her and my dad had to drag it back onto the property, where it was now laying – exactly as I had seen it in the dream. I did not understand how it was possible, but it was an event that stayed in my mind. It would take many pieces of the puzzle like this one before I could begin to see the larger picture God was trying to show me.

I had several of these kinds of dreams, the purpose of which was to train me to pay attention to my dreams and watch closely to see the results.

At this time in my life, I was struggling and suffering trying to find my purpose. It seemed as though I had tried many different professions and careers but they all ended in failure. I even struggled with knowing who I really was, and tried different kinds of lifestyles and friends but none of them fit well.

I had a long and difficult teenage life, many of those years having lived in isolation and faced a lifetime of rejection and bitterness. I was depressed for many years, and around this time everything came to a head. I began to sink into a depression that was the worst of my life, and being in my mid-20's, I began to look at those around me who seemed to be succeeding in life while I was remaining stagnant and unproductive.

One of my lifetime dreams was that I had always desired to have a lasting, loving marriage and have my own daughters one day. This was a dream that has been with me all my life, but as I looked around me I saw only loneliness, depression and the hopelessly bleak future I had staring back at me.

Late at night I would sit there at my window and look outside at the darkness. I would open the window even in the middle of winter. I wanted to see and hear the darkness and feel the coldness. This was my comfort, because I could relate to it so well. It was indifferent and unfeeling, it was cold and its presence was absolute. It was ominous and lorded over everyone, placing them under its feet. I longed to have a purpose, but I felt I was too deep or too far gone to climb out of the hole I was in.

As I looked outside, my neighbor's house seemed empty and dead. I always knew my neighbors and played with them as a child. I had fond memories of them; they were a staple in my childhood. We lived out in the country where your neighbors never changed, you knew the same people all your life and they were almost like family.

Recently however, our neighbors had a divorce and sold the house. It was as though even my memories and childhood was being stripped away and I could remember almost nothing joyous or happy about my past. It was long nights like these that plagued me everywhere I went, and every time I went to sleep.

I would sometimes talk to God. I would always ask why I suffer so much, and what was the true purpose of my life? I would pour my heart out to God, pleading for Him to listen to me. I was tired of being lonely and depressed. I did my best to stop serving the enemy and try to find my way to God. I was reading the bible and learning of the Word... but it was all lifeless and dead to me. I never heard God's voice; I did not understand how He worked. I couldn't figure out why everyone else seems to be alright but even though I do exactly what they do, I fail and do not succeed. This occurred time and time again. I would sit in my room alone, and mull over the situations in my life. I remember talking to God even when I could not feel Him, or sense Him. In the depth of my isolation the only choice I had was to talk and believe that God was hearing it.

My hopelessness peaked, and one night I lay in my bed ready to sleep. I felt I should talk to God again, as I always did at this point. But this time it was different. With tears streaming down my face, I would politely thank God for this life. I thanked Him for my family, my experiences, and the things I shared with others... and overall I guess I was pretty blessed with all things considered. I confessed that I didn't understand what it was all for, and contended with God about why I suffered so much in vain. I asked Him what my purpose was. However, after this many years, and the depth of hopelessness I was in, I just asked God to take me home now. I sincerely prayed with all my heart for a quiet and peaceful death. "I read that God was merciful, maybe now He would show it to me," is what I thought. I prayed this solid and persistent for 3 days and 3 nights. On the third night, as I cried myself to sleep after my earnest prayer, that is when The Lord God Almighty moved His Hand upon my life.

In this dream, I suddenly found myself standing in a city street. I was looking at the face of a church building, and I went inside. I sat down in a chair, and there were many people sitting inside the other chairs, looking around and talking. They were gossiping and talking about each other. Sitting in front of me was a couple who were in wheelchairs. Suddenly, the man stood up from his wheelchair and everyone looked astonished. But the man turned to his companion; also wheelchair bound, and said to her, “I deceived you so that I could be with you to get what I wanted. I pretended to be disabled, and I lied to you so that you would easily accept me and I could manipulate you.” I turned my attention toward the pulpit, and behind there was a staircase leading up to a door, and behind the door the stairs continued upwards and wrapped around to a second level. The door was opened, and a man in a very fine business suit came walking down the stairs and stood near the pulpit, with his hands folded in front of him. The man was extremely handsome, but he had the purest form of hatred and evil in his eyes. It was so strong, his mere presence made the air so thick you couldn't breathe. As I looked upon his face and into his eyes, the air was so heavy with evil that I collapsed onto the floor under the oppression of such pure evil.

I was taken out of the church, and found myself standing on a long straight road. I could see a city off in the distance, and an inner voice told me, “You are in California.” There were large fields on either side of the road. Suddenly, there was a massive earthquake that took place and it was so large and devastating, the Earth itself was swallowed up in certain places. I saw sinkholes form that looked like bottomless pits, some were larger than football fields. There were now many people running around in calamity near the fields and in the road. I remember seeing people driving very slowly in the road, scared that the weight of their car would break the road and swallow their car and themselves into the abyss. I was crawling on my hands and knees very slowly; testing the ground in front of me to make sure it wouldn't collapse, such as when soldiers search for land mines. The Earth was so fragile because of the magnitude of this earthquake. If it could be measured, it would be at least a 20.0

I saw a tow truck driver show up on the road. He was there to help and assist the other people who were stuck in their cars, those who were stranded in the middle of the disaster. He became very rude and abrasive and started to express his anger, and told people that he wasn't helping others even though he was equipped to do so. Suddenly I saw a Jewish man appear next to me, and I could not look upon His face. It was an intuition that told me He was Jewish. He asked the tow truck driver with compassion, “Why do you hate me?” The tow truck driver replied, “Because in the end, you people have always had a ticket out of here.” At this I felt like I was supposed to say something, as though they were both waiting for me to speak. I still had a choice to speak, and so I replied, “You know you can be saved too.” And then I woke up.

I felt anew as I woke up that morning, I pondered the dream I had, because it was very clear and very powerful. I decided to write it down because it was so vivid. It felt like God was revealing parts of the future to me, and illustrating the corruption within the churches these days, and giving a glimpse of His wrath. I felt that I encountered Jesus in that dream, and I felt such a perfect peace after I woke up. I began to have increasingly vivid dreams of this nature, and lengthier ones. One of the most powerful experiences I have had to date was a vision of Hell.

I lay down one night to sleep, and as I drifted off into sleep I began to dream in normal fashion. During the dream, I was outside flying on a bird when suddenly a portal opened up in the sky. It was a funnel, like an upside down tornado. I was pulled into this funnel, and as I traveled through it I began to wake up as I continued in this dream. It was more than a lucid dream, because in the past I have experienced lucidity in dreams but this was very different. It was more real. Everything was amplified, my senses more sensitive and accurate. I could hear more, see more, feel more, and the sense of time had disappeared altogether. There was no past, present, or future sense. On the inside of this funnel cloud, there were horrible looking creatures and figures that were stuck in the walls, or sides, of the funnel. Some were like human torsos with limbs trying to reach out and grab you.

As I entered the base of the funnel, I blacked out for a moment and awoke on a conveyor belt. My whole body was paralyzed, and I was fully awake and aware of what was happening to me. I was petrified with fear, I knew I was just in my bed sleeping a while ago, and very confused as to where I was at or what was happening to me. I could only look out of my eyes, and the place was very large. It was a long, straight conveyor belt that seemed to go on forever. The walls and ceiling of this room seemed to have infinite depth between them and myself. One of the first senses I could come to grips with was smell, because the stench of this place was so putrid. It smelled like death, burnt flesh and decaying matter.

I saw a figure standing off in the distance, and at first I thought it might have been Jesus, or maybe I just wished it was, because I was very scared and everything I was experiencing was more real than reality itself. My vision started to dissipate and my eyes were closed, after a moment I was able to reopen them again and the figure was standing a little bit closer, but still about 30 feet away. Again, my vision faded and my eyes closed. After another moment, I was able to open my eyes once more and saw the figure closer still, this time only about 15 feet away. The process repeated itself, and then it was standing beside me. It was very tall, about 10 feet in height and it was also very skinny. Its arms hung down to around the knee level. Its head was enlarged, and it was emanating a strong wave of pure fear. I felt that fear, and it penetrated every sense I had. I was scared for my life... I kept calling out for Jesus, but to no avail.

Suddenly, this demon bent over very quickly until its face came to touch mine. Instantly, it disappeared and the conveyor belt started moving. As I was being moved along the belt, the demon resurfaced and was walking beside me. It had very long strides between each step, and with each step, its body sunk down low and rose up again. It was all so real, every detail, and all my senses were amplified. I was in pure terror and fear. I knew my family was above me, on the surface of the Earth, going about their usual business. I missed them, I wanted to warn them, I wanted to escape this place but I never entertained the thought because escape was impossible. I somehow knew I was in the center of the Earth while all this was going on.

As the demon walked alongside me, I began to cry out for Jesus. The demon laughed at me, and continued to laugh each time I called upon the name of Jesus. The conveyor belt began to take me into a very small space, almost like one of those ventilation shafts or air ducts you see spies crawling through in the movies. The ceiling part, which was only about 6 inches away from my face, was composed of individual blocks that were as wide as the space I was in, but about 3 Inch segments. So, there must have been about 24 blocks for the length of my 6 foot body. They all moved independently from one another, also. The blocks began to move by themselves, one at a time, to come down and crush whatever was on the conveyor belt – me. I began to feel a fear that I cannot put into words because this was all reality to me, everything was real and the fear seemed to have no end. Just when I thought I could not be more afraid and helpless, something greater happened to instill more fear. However, when the blocks came down to crush each section of my body flat, they were not allowed to touch me. But I knew their purpose, and if they could, they would hurt me and torment me and I would feel all the pain. It never dawned on me why they didn't crush me, because the fear was so overwhelming I could not think straight or process any kind of logic or reasoning. I came out of this machine, and back into open space again where the demon appeared once more beside me. I was able to turn my head to the left, and I began to see a large and long line of people. They looked so sad, so desperate, so hopeless... and to their right side was a large open window in the wall. As I looked outside the window it looked exactly like the surface of Mars. It was a reddish brown tint, and the entire landscape was barren and devoid of all life. There was no water, no moisture. I looked at the line of people, and I said to myself, "Oh no... I prayed for these people, and I didn't want them to come here...". At this, the demon knew my thoughts and cackled maniacally as it replied, "There is no hope here. Now these next ones will cut you".

The conveyor belt took me inside another machine, exactly similar to the previous one except these blocks had sharp razors on them. Once more, they came down to cut me into pieces, and I feared them because I have been in this place for some time now, fully aware of where I am and what this place means. However, they were only allowed to prick me and not cut me. After I came out of this machine, the demon reappeared beside me and walked with me. I screamed and cried out for Jesus, but the demon only laughed harder and harder. He laughed so hard at me that it scared me, but then he turned to me and said, "You'll see Him next". I immediately woke up after this statement.

Saints, after waking up from this very alive and real experience, I was unable to sleep or eat for a period of time. I can tell you from the experience that God is real, Jesus is real, and Hell is real. You are in a battle, and you are either soldiers for God or soldiers for satan. There is no gray area in this at all, as Jesus Himself clearly states in Matthew 12:30 (NIV), "He who is not with me is against me, and he who does not gather with me scatters ..."

Over time, God began to reveal to me that He was showing me parts of the future. I believe in my very first dream God was showing his anger towards the corruption in His churches. I saw California destroyed by the largest earthquake in history. God is very angry towards America and her harlot ways, and His grace is being lifted from the churches across this nation.

I was shown another vision one night, and in it I was standing outside my home in the driveway. It began to rain, but not with water. It was raining tiny pebbles and rocks but they were falling with extreme velocity. When they hit the ground, they penetrated about 3 inches deep into the soil. I looked up to the sky, and the atmosphere turned red. I watched as the sun was covered in sackcloth and darkened, and the stars fell out of the sky. The moon also turned red like blood. I walked unharmed towards the back of my property, where there was a wide and deep view of the horizon. I could see many miles of distance, lots of hills and fields as far as the eye could see. There were smaller meteors that were falling through the atmosphere around me, and it was all so real. I could see them crash, and there was a delay before I heard the sound and it resonated throughout me and my surroundings. All physics applied to this vision and it was very vivid. Suddenly, I saw a massive asteroid descend upon the Earth and it collided with massive force. I watched in total disbelief and horror as I saw the light first and heard the sound later. It literally peeled the Earth's crust back in a ripple effect as a water droplet does in a large bowl. I thought to myself, "that is going to reach here eventually…" in awe I just stood there watching, and thought to myself again, "here it is, this is it… this is really the end". As the blast wave and fire storm from this impact approached me, I ran around the opposite side of my house thinking that it would somehow protect me. As I crouched down on my porch, I saw the blast go by me and heard the destruction and even felt the heat of the fire. Giant walls of flame wrapped around the house to try and embrace me and engulf me. However, there was a shield around me that I could see and the fire could not touch me at all.

When the firestorm dissipated and the dust settled, I walked out from my porch and looked around about me. Everything was destroyed and laid to waste. There were some foundations left, broken buildings, and smoldering pits of fire. I was surprised there was even this much left. I remember thinking, "This is how we live now. It is every man for himself; dog eat dog, lawlessness and anarchy. There is no grace anymore and no hope". I remember going into the basement of our house and I was there with my family. We had to hide here and protect ourselves from any other survivors. We lived in a world without God's Grace. After this, I woke up.

God once spoke to me and told me that I will bring forth bad news to give to the people. He also said that I would face much rejection, because people will not want to believe what messages I bring. The adversity and challenges I faced in my life have shaped me into who I am today, able to withstand the enemy through Christ, and allow God to use me in any way He desires. But I have chosen of my own free will to do this for God, and in doing so, by warning the people of what is to come and to find salvation at the cross – their blood is not on my hands.

If God has called you, and chosen you, you must understand that God will use each person differently. He will actually use your personality and attributes to work through you. My Pastor, Barbara Lynch, is a mentor and true shepherd for the Lord. She has helped me greatly in learning the deeper truths of the Word. God placed me on the path to Delaware to be under her tutor-age; and I give all thanks to God, and have great respect for His chosen servants. God used her strong willed personality to assist me in being delivered from bondage which was deeply rooted. She is a true champion on the faith, and God knew this. It was under her guidance, and that of the Holy Spirit, that I was able to understand the calling on my life and how to serve God in truth and in spirit.

God never goes against our will, and He will only be able to use what we yield to Him. In some of us, God can use the parts within us that are yielded, and in others, God will only use them if they are completely yielded to Him. I am trying to illustrate that it is all up to God who is used, when, to what length and purpose, and it is God alone by His Grace that calls and chooses us. There is nothing we can do to earn or deserve a single thing from God. Is God calling you? Has He chosen you? Are you asking for

His will each morning and seeking His face for all your decisions? Are you completely yielded to God 100 percent or just 99.9? If you are missing even one rung in the ladder, you will not be able to take the next step to where God wants you to be. We are in a season and dispensation where it is literally all or nothing, saints. Either you die to yourself and live for Christ in all ways every day or you lose out.

The times will be difficult and test each of us to our core. These are the end times we are living in, right now. And yes, it really is all or nothing. Many people will give up or be unwilling to surrender 100 percent of themselves to God, and therefore fall by the wayside. Jesus knew it would be this way in the end times, as He posed this question to His followers in Luke 18:8 (NIV), "... However, when the Son of Man comes, will he find faith on the earth?"

One night I had a vision that took me up into a part of Heaven. I was standing in a very large white room. Absolutely everything was white. The whole place shone brighter than the sun, and as I looked around I noticed it was a courtroom. I saw the bench, the tables, the seats, etc. I could not see the judge Himself because it was too bright; but I absolutely knew He was there.

Before me was a very, VERY long line of people I knew in my lifetime. They were all lined up shoulder-to-shoulder, the line was growing and going on forever to my left side. I was not sure what was about to take place or what was happening, but to my absolute dread I soon found out where I was and what was happening.

The first person stepped forward, and I was there before them. Suddenly, one by one, every single solitary word I spoke about them, to them, behind them, around them; every single thing I ever did to them, in the open or in secret; every single thing I even thought about them, or *felt* about them, was brought forth into the light. That person standing before me saw, knew, felt, and experienced everything I did to them even my most secret thoughts were brought into the light. I was forced to stand in front of them in plain view as they reacted to everything that was brought to light.

I felt massive guilt and embarrassment. I felt total complete shame and disgrace, absolute humiliation. Every lie I spoke was revealed. Every dark thought was brought to light and made known to that person. And I knew that I had to start at the beginning of my life and deal with this person until every single thing was revealed. Then after that eternity of embarrassment, it would be on to person #2. And so on, and so on.

Mercifully, I was awoken shortly after. But as I woke up, I carried into my waking reality the same heaviness of shame and humiliation. It took several hours to shake off those feelings and return to 'normal'. But I will never shake off the lesson gleaned from this vision: Everything you say, do, think and feel towards others will absolutely be revealed and made known to all. This is the judgment we must all go through in the final days. God will truly bring all darkness into light. And no one thing is ever hidden from God. Everyone will be judged. This was God's message to me to take to the people. Heed this vision and apply these principles to your life; treat others as though everything you do will be made known to all people.

In June of 2011, I had another vision of hell. I was inside a large warehouse, but I lay on a conveyor belt again. Every 10 seconds my head would ache, and I heard a sound like a long dull noise. This lasted for 10 seconds and disappeared for 10 seconds. Then, the Holy Spirit said to me, "They do this to look inside your mind, they want to see your thoughts".

The conveyor belt that I am on has a large mirror in front of me and a large mirror behind me, so that all I can see is just a reflection of myself infinitely. In addition, at that time the Holy Spirit spoke again, "They have you here, they are inside everyone's thoughts now, and they are trying to find something".

I fought so hard to get off this conveyor belt and out from between these two large mirrors. After an intense struggle of making my muscles move, I was able to stand up. I had gotten off the conveyor belt but as I tried to walk away, I could only take very small steps. There was an invisible force making me weak and trying to place me back on the conveyor belt. As this was happening, I noticed one of my eyes was forced closed and I could not open it. I felt as though it was asleep, and I had to wake it up so that I could open it and see clearly in order to escape this place. I began to use my fingers to attempt to forcibly open my closed eye, and I keep shouting: "I'm awake! I'm awake! I need to move!" and then I had finally opened my eye and broken free.

I ran out from the warehouse area and through some hallways and corridors. I eventually came to a washroom and I hid inside one of the stalls. I began to pray to Jesus asking Him, "Please Lord... keep them from me..." but then I saw a black shadow moving fast near me; it moved very fast and it could go through walls, and as it got closer to me it was pure black. I knew it was evil, I could feel it... then suddenly, it took hold of me and it put me on another conveyor belt. And again the Holy Spirit spoke, "This one goes to a different place. This is the one for people who are strong and try to break free."

The new conveyor belt took me to an underground place. I could see we were going into caverns and still deeper into the center of the Earth. It looked like a dangerous crazy-factory where there are chains, pipes, platforms and there's molten lava here. I saw some people being tortured here, and I assumed the creatures I saw here were demons but they had humanoid forms. They are incredibly tall and very large, the sight of them shocked me. They are at least 8 feet tall and weigh 900lbs but they can walk upright and fast. They were very flexible and agile despite their physical build. They are also maliciously violent and filled with hatred, as I discerned from watching them and their behavior.

I noticed a chain around me, and the other end was held by one of these demons. No sooner than I noticed it, the demon cast me down into the lava but I did not feel any pain. I once again had divine protection. Then I was taken out of the lava and brought to a platform with one of the demons. It was walking around me, glaring at me, and finally it asked me in a loud intimidating voice, "WHERE IS THE ONE WHO LIVES IN FIRE? THE ONE WHO'S HANDS ARE STAINED WITH BLOOD AND SULFUR?". Their voices spoke with power to rob you of all hope. It was like a thunder that shook your soul down to the foundation – and shattered it. I knew that time, by the Holy Spirit, "It is asking of the devil. They all want to know where the devil, their dark king, is." I said to the demon, "He is in the center of the Earth, in hell." At this, the large demon was filled with absolute rage. It was more than anger, it was absolute rage. He threw me, but I was protected. I remember looking up through a hallway, an even larger demon, similar to the others, was slumping through the door. It was at least 12 feet tall and weighed maybe more than a ton. But it was pregnant, as I saw a fetus inside of its stomach. I had the impression something was about to be birthed into the world that is straight from the throne of hell.

Upon waking from this dream, I knew that I am in the true end times. I believe as though the enemy is being birthed into this world in this generation, even mocking the conception and birth of our Lord Jesus and counterfeiting God's entrance to this world with his own perverted methods.

2011 was a rough year for me. It felt like many things were being taken away from me and that doors were being closed all around me. It had been several years that I was having recurring dreams of airplanes crashing near my home and in my back yard, with supernaturally large explosions following. These particular dreams increased in length and intensity as time moved forward closer to the middle of 2011. It transitioned into a weekly, and almost a daily occurrence. Planes would be crash landing, free falling near me or chasing me. At the time I did not understand the interpretation of those dreams, but it was as though I was being chased out of my home that I had lived in all the days of my life.

One of the most vivid dreams I had was when I was standing in my bedroom looking out my window. I saw flood waters coming through my neighborhood and I was staring at the scenery noticing how every house and every tree was standing out in great detail. As the waters rose higher, I thought to myself the neighbors are going to have their homes ruined because they were on a lower elevation than I was.

A small wave appeared and washed over some of the front lawns and cars in the distance, and the waters kept rising. A second wave which was much taller came and washed over houses closer to me, and again a third wave came and flooded our driveway and came up to the window on the first floor.

Suddenly, all the water began to recede. I heard the storm drains in the streets gurgle and bubble with air, and then a moment later a massive tidal wave that was 3 times taller than our house came and snapped trees like toothpicks and was fast approaching the house. I turned and ran out of my room and down the stairs. I heard a loud crash and glass breaking, wood snapping, houses collapsing – and I looked back to see tree branches mixed with flood water bust open the door to my bedroom as I was being forced out of my room and out of my home. After this, I woke up.

Chapter 4: Being Born Again

In reality, I was being led to leave my home in Rhode Island. A family member offered to have me live with him and his wife in Virginia. At the present time I mulled over my options. The more I thought about it, I had very little opportunities left in Rhode Island. I had a sudden empowerment and ambition that I could not explain as the time drew nearer to decide before my deadline. I eventually chose to move out of my home and comfort zone to try something new.

I must take a moment to reflect on my past at this juncture. As I look back, writing this and thinking in retrospect, I am elated and overjoyed to express my understanding of God's love. Our God is truly long-suffering and patient. I have learned that He would not go against my free will, and that many of my actions and choices created paths I had to walk down – ones that God never desired me to go down – but as God, He ultimately turns all evil around for our good and His Glory.

I was receiving so many dreams and visions from God and yet I never understood them. I did not ever hear or believe that God could show me things because He loves me, and has a purpose for my life. I never believed or was taught that God gives us each a mission before we are born and it is up to us to discover and seek that purpose and then be responsible for bringing it forth in this world. We are truly children of God in every sense. Some of us have higher or deeper callings than others, as the bible says, many are called but few are chosen.

God's love in its most pure and ultimate form is unthinkable and incomprehensible. Its power and potency has literally destroyed circumstances and problems within my life. There have been times that God has sent His love as a touch that affects me so deeply I will burst into tears no matter where I am and collapse to the ground feeling the most complete peace that surpasses all understanding. There have been times that someone has been laid on my heart and I suddenly weep heavily over them for no apparent reason. But this is God allowing me to feel His heart for that person... and it opens a door for me to pray for that person and the Holy Spirit leads me in such powerful prayer that was divinely appointed.

Though we cannot see God, we can see His love for us in a multitude of ways. His love is best expressed in those individuals who have completely yielded themselves to Him. A good tree will bare good fruit, and a bad tree will produce bad fruit. It is true with people today also.

Now, in this juncture of my life I had just made a decision to relocate myself and try a new life in Virginia. I literally packed all I had in my little two-door Saturn, and was able to drive the 430 miles without many problems. (I could write another book about how God has kept my car together.) After arriving in Virginia I acclimated quite well to the area and was pleased with the positive changes I experienced while going through a culture shock. Yes, the north is quite different than the mid-Atlantic in some respects.

Despite a refreshing change in my life, I still struggled with many issues within and around myself. I was continuing to have difficulty moving forward and understanding what I was supposed to be doing with myself. My family that I was living with was attempting to help me grow and conform to the secular world, to increase my responsibilities and accountability for myself.

I seemed to have an inner blockage that prevented me from thinking clearly as to what was priority, and what was not. I was faced with a deadline to attain a job or face the possibility of living in a homeless shelter. Again, the dark reality of going nowhere had caused all types of emotion to swirl around within me.

After much searching I finally landed a job that allowed me to save enough money in the first 2 months to afford my own apartment. This was a big step for me, because this time I was doing it by myself. My family assisted me in finding a place to live and I was very quickly moved into my new apartment which was in West Virginia.

Many changes happened very quickly, and yet at this time I kept asking God what was happening to me. I did not understand God, or what was happening. God didn't speak to me about my situation either. At this point everything was a total faith walk.

I had become dependent on other people due to my lifestyle, and because of this, it made it difficult to adapt and manage things on my own. It felt like a sink-or-swim scenario, and almost unbearable, but I would later come to realize these types of predicaments would occur more frequently in my future! I found the stress and pressures of life becoming greater and greater.

While I was managing to get by, I was not prospering as I should and I was not yet in the perfect will of God. More refining was necessary for me to be in the place God wanted and needed me to be at.

I maintained my job while I moved from Virginia to West Virginia. The commute was a long one but I did what I had to do, all the while I felt like I was not stable. I felt like I kept moving and drifting farther away from my family. I was struggling and barely making it by. I was surviving off scrap food and fast food dollar menus.

In my apartment, I had an inflatable air mattress for a bed, a computer desk and a chair as the only furniture I owned. It was quite comical to see it, but I never invited anyone over anyway. I questioned what it was God was doing with me and why I seemed to be going further down a hole rather than discovering my true self and potential.

You see, I had in my mind that a secular existence and purpose was the only thing I was supposed to have. I was supposed to work every day doing things I didn't want to do, just to scrape by and have enough for myself. This was my mindset, and it wasn't something I looked forward to.

Now when everything was most fragile, when it seemed like my life was hanging by its last thread, that is when I lost my job.

I couldn't pay my lease, I didn't have gas for my car, and I never once went food shopping the entire time I lived in West Virginia. I didn't have the money for it. I only made three paychecks at this job before I paid a security deposit and first month's rent, and had to buy appliances and necessities to live. This is when I knew I was hitting rock bottom.

I was hundreds of miles away from my family. I had no job, and couldn't find any new work. I had no money and no food... I was behind on bills and was about to be evicted from my apartment. I wasn't having any dreams or visions and no insight at all. I felt lost and helpless, but I continued to cry out to God. But no matter how much time passed or what pain I endured, I was not seeing or hearing anything at all from the God I believed in. This was my most uncertain and trying time in my faith, and I honestly felt abandoned.

It was around Christmas time and I had nothing, except for a package my mother and father had sent me so that I could have at least some food and a present to lift my mood. My parents had offered to take me back to their home in Rhode Island because of my desperate situation but I politely declined. In my mind I felt like I wanted to push this as far and hard as I could until the bitter end before I gave up. I felt like I had to do something different this time, instead of falling back in a safety net. I wanted to sink or swim.

I had extended family that lived in Delaware, and one of them called me and invited me to their house for Christmas dinner because they knew that I was not doing anything where I was. At the time, I did not tell them about my circumstances because I was slightly embarrassed about it. I drove a few hundred miles to get there and I was able to see some of the rest of my family there. I asked my family member about the church that he goes to because it had caught my interest in past conversations. It was a prophetic church, which was something different than I'm used to. I had really only been to church once or twice in my lifetime and each one was more of a larger sized church that appealed to the masses. At that time, I didn't know what God's anointing felt like and I couldn't discern which church had a portion of it and which ones didn't.

Upon my first visit to the church, I received my first prophetic word. It was a strange thing to me at first, having a prophet talk to me and speak the Word of God from His throne of Grace. But what struck me is that this prophet knew things about me that no one else knew, and I was not from this area where anyone could know me. She spoke directly into my life and about my past, and declared all of the things which God would have me do in my lifetime and how He would use my past experiences to further His kingdom. I knew it was God speaking to me through this prophet because to suggest otherwise would be an impossibility given the foreknowledge they had and insight into my life. To say it was not of God must acknowledge the presence of a higher intelligence with all-knowing capabilities. That in itself is an acknowledgment of God.

In these words of wisdom that were spoken over me, I began to see a truth coming from the words themselves. I started to read the Word of God in the bible and the words would minister to me about what love is and how God worked through the world and it revealed more of who He is. Within the testimonies and accounts of the bible we can begin to see who God is and how He works. The words are alive, they have life to them. They live and grow within us as we receive them into our spirits.

Chapter 5: The First Assignment

It was nearly impossible for me to travel back and forth between West Virginia and Delaware every weekend, and while I was visiting in Delaware I had a talk with my family member. I had explained my situation and he agreed with family that I could stay and live there with him. It was a humbling experience for me because I was already being moved around several times and now had to bunk in with another side of my family. At the time I did not understand what was happening, other than my luck seemed to be down and out and I began to feel like a failure.

As I kept returning to this church, the Pastor continued to speak over me what the Lord would say. At first I was skeptical of these things, even though the words spoke about my past and my future and seemed to be accurate. I was uneasy about believing such things, especially being in a state of depression seeking some kind of acceptance. But you will see as we go forward how everything that prophet spoke over me came to pass and became reality within the year of 2012.

I discovered that learning more about God was a struggle, because what I expected to hear and receive was not exactly what God was giving me. I was told by God to write a book, this book, and to do His work first. My pastor had shared with me that she felt as though a secular job was not right for me at the time despite my circumstances – because it felt as though this book God had asked me to write, and future ones, would be my livelihood. Many people did not understand the choices I was making as I did what I thought was best to align myself with what I believed God wanted me to do. In the world, people would go of their own will into the secular workforce to support themselves as their first course of action if they were in a situation similar to mine. However, because of the dreams and visions I had been having, and the words God spoke over me, I had to live a very unique way of life doing things people did not expect me to do. God had even warned me that many people would not understand me or the choices I make, and many would not even listen to the things that I have to say.

The challenge was being asked questions by people who did not understand the depth of obedience to God, even to the point of homelessness. Too many people have religious mindsets, and think that God won't do certain things. But in all truth, if God wants to make you homeless to teach you something that will build you up in Him, then it is His prerogative to do so. If God wants to place you in other people's lives as a burden, perhaps you are not the one being tested.

I want to tell you about who God is and how He works. Let my life story be as an example to you of servant-hood, and wisdom. God sent me to Delaware to live in a unique condition that I struggled with. It was not easy for me to battle various elements associated with my living conditions, and some nights I cried out to God to take me away from that place… it became an emotional battle and struggle to even eat or bathe at the place I was moved into.

Since all of us went to the same church, we all had the same idea of what the Lord God has asked us to do in our lives. Some of the people I lived around were asked to love me as Christ loves; and to welcome me into their home. Some of them did this, and as time went on, some of the love disappeared. My unique calling was confusing people around me, leading them to come against me and speak against me. It was a culmination of pressures, accusations, and otherwise uncomfortable variables and struggles that lead me to choose where I lay my head. Finally, I had just given up hope and couldn't bear to stay at this place any longer. I asked my Pastor for permission to stay at the church temporarily, and she said yes. The members of church provided food for me, and some spare money for gasoline.

There had come a time when my pastor came to me and prophesied over me a word from God that had said I was ready to move on. It was time for me to move into another home. I replied and asked my pastor why did God allow me to suffer so greatly?

Then God prophesied through her and asked me, “Why are you complaining? You served your purpose: you were a test for those around you – to reveal the condition of their hearts.” In other words, I need to take up my cross and follow Jesus as the word says and do so without complaining. My suffering was irrelevant, because the purpose of all this was to test the hearts of those around me. Just as God tested Abraham – God tests us to see if our hearts are sincere and truly desire to do His will at all cost.

God then spoke over me to tell me that my experience in all this had been my very first assignment. The people being tested had failed, and now it was time to use me elsewhere. My second assignment was to be placed in a home with a drug addict to minister to him. At the time of moving into this home, living with my uncle and aunt, it fulfilled one of the prophecies that was spoken over me several months beforehand when I first arrived in Delaware.

You must understand that God cannot go against our free will. There is a system behind everything that is done. There is God’s perfect will, and below that is God’s permissive will, and below that is God’s tests and trials to bring you back up to His perfect will. Think of it like a GPS system that has your destination already mapped out. It has already calculated your most effective and efficient route, taking into consideration the avoidance of construction and tolls. If you are doing well following the route at that time, but then you happen to get distracted and miss your exit ramp, the GPS must recalculate a different route for you. Ultimately it will be leading to your final destination but it might have you go a longer or more congested route. This analogy can be applied in our walks with God. Sometimes we make mistakes that take us out of the will of God and that causes problems for us – because it's not the road God ever intended for us to go down!

Yes, God is long-suffering, but He also has emotions and feelings as the human heart does. God can feel anger, love, jealousy, etc. God knows if your heart is hardened and you will never change and therefore sets you on a path of destruction. His love is always there, but His grace can be removed at times and for a season. An example of such people whose hearts are hardened and destined to destruction are Pharaoh and Judas Iscariot.

How God treats us is proportionate to the depth of the calling God has placed on our lives. I'm not talking about His love for us – His love is immeasurable and unconditional for all people. However, His grace is measured according to each person by His choosing. God may be very strict for one person, but very lenient for others. It depends on how deeply God wants to use you and how tightly you must walk the rope He has set before you. God is real and alive – we are made in His image. The things we experience, think and feel are extremely small and limited portions of how God Himself feels and thinks.

In my particular walk, I have been given dreams and visions and prophesies that showed exactly how God is treating me, which happens to be quite strict. God has revealed to me that this is the case because of the depth of the calling on my life. I have been told by God that I still do not understand the depth of the calling He has placed upon me. And if my vivid dreams of the future events are any indication of how I will be used then it is quite great indeed. Most of my dreams have come to pass, and in some cases I kept them privately to myself not even having written them down – and I was prophesied almost exactly as the dream showed. This was done to increase my faith in my seer anointing and the prophetic anointing.

Discovering these things was a long and complicated process. God lead me through many trials and circumstances to bring about these realizations to me. The revelation of these things of God came to me only through an open and obedient heart. It was because my circumstances around me were causing me to lower myself and humble myself more and more, which as the Word of God says is the way to become closer with God. As the first will be last and the last will be first.

Sometimes as we follow God and do the things He has asked us to do, we find ourselves trapped in daily life and circumstances. These issues that surface and test us can easily distract us and cause us to stumble and fall. The Word tells us that circumstances are menial and unimportant. Look at Paul, who struggled with a particular thorn in his flesh; yet God would not remove it at the time. God simply said that His grace was sufficient. Here was a man that was persecuted and chained in prison, yet praised God with the joy of the Lord as his strength. How many of us are locked in stocks and bonds in a roman prison and continue to praise God and trust Him? Sometimes the smallest things in our lives, such as gossip or someone slandering us at church, is enough to distract us and take us away from God's path and righteousness. How many people in today's society and age would endure thorns of the flesh which seem like giant cutting blades rather than small wooden specks? When God searches the Earth for open and obedient hearts, will He find men like Paul?

Living for God is not just surrendering our ways so we can feel good and be rewarded. We should genuinely surrender our ways, wants and desires simply because God is God and He is who He is; without expectation of return. When you center your heart on this mindset, nothing can shake you or take you off the path that God has set before you. Jesus is our perfect example for all situations in life. He listened only for the voice of His Father in Heaven and did only what He told him to say and do. Jesus also struggled with the flesh, as we all do, and at times He would be overwhelmed. At times such as these, He would go away to the mountaintop to pray alone with His Father for wisdom and discernment. We must follow this example so that we can have the correct guidance to solve our problems in life.

The Word of God has the answer to all of our problems in life. I have not yet found an issue in the daily lives of people that has not been addressed in some form or another in the Bible. How do we find the answers we seek? Some of this requires active participation in the Word; we must be daily searching and striving to learn and apply what we learn. With prayer, asking God to lead us to scriptures that can teach us Godly principles and minister to our specific life issues, we can then learn how to properly handle the most challenging and deep struggles life tries to place upon our backs. Solving problems according to the Word helps keep us on the primary route that God has calculated for us on our spiritual GPS devices.

Letting God take control of our lives sounds like quite a daunting task. But really it doesn't need to be as complicated as it sounds. If we exercise the fruits of the Spirit, living according to the guidelines the bible tells us to live, we should be so close to God in an intimate relationship that we can easily hear the still small voice in our hearts. Being intimate with God means that we can feel His heart and know His thoughts throughout the day. It is possible to be so close with God that people will find it difficult to see where you end and God begins. There have been many times when God has placed feelings in my heart and caused me to weep over a person without warning or any logical reason. After weeping, I would pray and ask God why I felt this way. The Lord would tell me that He has shared His heart with me, and what I felt just then was what He feels for them. Sometimes God just wants us to share His heart, and other times He causes us to feel His heart for a particular person so that we can pray for them. God works in mysterious ways... but this all requires us to be walking so closely with Him. God wants us to strive daily to live a holy lifestyle. The Word tells us that a righteous man falls seven times, but gets back up seven times. As humans we will fall and stumble, but what makes us righteous is repenting sincerely and moving forward and doing warfare to prevent the enemy's lies from dragging us back into sin.

To understand the love of God better, let us look in Jeremiah chapter 5. God challenges anyone to find but one person who is upright and honest, living a holy lifestyle. If even one can be found, God would spare the entire city. This can also be applied to our homes. I have known families where only one person in that household truly serves God and lives in the battle of holy living. Even the sinners in the home are protected and blessed because of the one member of the family who is Christ-like.

When we face trials and persecution in life we must pray and discern where they have come from. I have heard of many pastors and believers who assume someone is living in sin because they have become ill or laden with many burdens. This can be a mistake! In the book of Job, his closest friends accused him rather than comforted him. In actuality, the Lord God handed Job over to Satan by asking him if he had 'considered' His servant Job. These trials came from God Himself, having allowed them to happen, having known Job's heart would not forsake God. In the end, Job was blessed with twice as much as he had in the beginning. However, there are times when our trials have come from Satan because he convinced us to pick up burdens that God never desired for us to pick up – this happens all the time when we step out of God's will and do our own will. The key to correcting this particular issue is to get before God and sincerely repent. By asking God to forgive us, and then moving forward in faith and listening for the voice of God to lead us through the trials we must now endure, our disobedience can be worked through and eventually overcome. God will always be there beside us to walk us through it. How much you must suffer through is dependent on how quickly you truly repent and seek to do God's will over your own.

Chapter 6: The Second Assignment

My first assignment was not made known to me until it was over. I would like to share that God will sometimes remain silent in regards to answering your prayers; because if He told you everything you were asking about, you might not do what He is asking you to do and to go through what He is trying to bring you through. Sometimes we must walk by faith and not by sight. At this point I had been living in the church every day, the conditions there were more favorable over the living quarters I was placed in previously. I was used to washing my clothes in the bathroom sink and taking bird baths. Some of the church members gave me food to eat, and sometimes money for gas.

Up until now I had mostly been depressed because of where I lived, because I had an expectation and a standard set up in my mindset that was far above where I was. I began to grow content with where I was at, in the sense of being joyful that I was not on the streets.

At this time, my pastor (who is my aunt, by marriage) invited me to live in her home. She had a home that was like a refuge, there were several people living there with her that she was aiding and she has always opened her home to the needy. She sat down with me and explained to me that God had me on my first assignment, and God had bluntly asked me why I was complaining about the last several months of my life? God explained that it was never about me at all – that everything I went through was only to reveal the hearts of those around me. The people whom I was sent to were asked to love me and care for me as Christ would – and the outcome was determined. Since it was final, it was time for me to move on to my second assignment. This time I would be ministering to a drug addict who lived in the home. With my past, it would be fitting for me to do the ministering – God knew what He was doing and He knew where to place me and when to place me there.

This man was a person who once grew up in church and knew the Word of God but had backslidden. With my background of drug abuse it would make me suitable to minister to him about how God had supernaturally delivered me from drugs.

In my past, I was addicted to pills. In one day I would consume 80mg of Oxycontin with 80mg of Vicodin. I also had smoked a pack of cigarettes a day, along with quite a bit of marijuana. I had done this for years, and it was a fairly dedicated practice. My tolerance was so high that I increasingly used more pills to get me through the day.

One day, God touched me – and I knew it was Him. I felt a total peace wash over me, a feeling of freedom and enlightenment. I felt like I had a new form of wisdom, a new leading and direction. It all happened suddenly in one day, and ever since that day that I felt the Holy Spirit inside of me I have not taken a single pill. There were absolutely no withdrawal symptoms and no urges whatsoever. I even stopped smoking cold turkey with ease, the mere smell of smoke made me ill. Something like this, where you see medical cases of habit-forming drugs and addictions, and severe cases of withdrawals – to all be eliminated in one day? There is no explanation for the most indescribable feeling of peace that can erase addiction other than a God of Love.

As time proceeded I began to befriend the people in this home, and start to learn their lifestyle and habits. It was an interesting and diverse bunch, but that was something I was used to being around in my life. I was treated with hospitality and warmth which was something I was craving and glad to have. I felt relieved knowing and understanding what had happened to me previously in my first assignment. It gave me a comfort and a peace when I understood what was happening. But in retrospect, sometimes we many never understand the reasons why things happen to us – and at those times we are walking by faith alone. And I would surely have situations like these in the days to come.

The man I was ministering to was on methadone at a high level dosage, and was smoking synthetic cannabis. Each night he would go through symptoms and side effects that were horrible to watch. He would start to feel nauseated and begin to vomit. Once he started vomiting, he was unable to stop for hours. He would sweat profusely and have violent body tremors, he would get extremely hot and cold intermittently, all the while vomiting and dry heaving for hours with painful headaches and stomach cramps. He also suffered with restless leg syndrome.

He would be in a state of fear each night, to the point he forced himself to wake up every hour. He felt that if he slept longer than an hour or two, he would get sick every time and begin the long process of torment with the episodes. He would ask us to call the ambulance each time he became violently ill, and made at least 3 trips to the hospital each week. The doctors would sometimes give him nausea medicine and send him out the door, which he claimed worked, but eventually the doctors and staff saw him only as a drug addict and neglected treating him and eventually barred him from the hospital.

At times when we were awakened by his cries at night, we would go and lay hands on him and pray for healing and speak peace over him. At times this helped, and at times God would speak to us about the situation – which is between him and God – and at times I began to see things that astonished me. God had anointed me earlier in the year with a seer anointing. Because of this I was able to see into the spirit realm and discern spirits and see them. On a particular night I witnessed such a vision as I saw him complain of stomach pains – I saw two small black demons, one clinging to the front of his stomach and another clinging to the back of his spine. These two demons had daggers in their hands, the first one thrust its dagger deeply into his back, and as it pulled it back out the other demon thrust its dagger deep into his stomach. This motion repeated itself endlessly. They disappeared and I saw only the man in pain and I began to pray against those spirits that were tormenting him.

Sometimes we cannot understand why God will heal one person and not another. I prayed constantly for God to heal this man in the same way that I was healed and delivered from all drugs, smoking and withdrawals. It did not happen like this, and that is solely up to the will of God whether or not it happens in this way.

There are also several factors that must be taken into consideration, such as any active sin in our lives that would prevent God's healing from coming forth – or even people that we are involved with that would hold us back or destroy us spiritually. Sometimes God will not heal us quickly or at all, as it can be designed to bring us to a place where we recognize that God is God, and He is the One who should order our footsteps.

Chapter 7: Words of Wisdom

We live in much more than the world we see around us. We only see the physical realm in which all of our laws of physics apply – where our immediate senses dominate and rule our logic. But I am telling you that there is a much larger spirit realm around about you. Ephesians 6:12 (NIV) says, "For our struggle is not against flesh and blood, but against the rulers, against the authorities, against the powers of this dark world and against the spiritual forces of evil in the heavenly realms." There is active warfare around you everywhere you go. The Word teaches us to love one another as we ought to love ourselves and not sin against one another. Jesus teaches us to love one another regardless of what we do – to love the person, but hate the sin itself. Sometimes people choose of their own free will to sin, while other times the enemy and his army leads us astray and puts thoughts and suggestions into our minds and hearts – that if these thoughts and imaginations are not dealt with immediately by spiritual warfare, they will become choices we willingly make and lead us into sin and darkness.

The enemy sends his minions out to make these suggestions to us, and creates assignments for his demons to set traps for the children of God to cause us to stumble and fall, or to keep us bound and confused, anything to keep us away from God or to prevent us from going any further with God. I have always told people that Satan doesn't need to convince you to follow him, he only needs to keep you out of the Will of God and he's won.

One of the greatest deceptions of the enemy is that once you are saved you are always saved. This is a lie from hell, and your salvation has to be worked out every second of every day. We have seen too many people have death experiences, and have visions, or prophetic words to confirm that God has chosen certain people to taste death and find themselves in hell, when they believed they were going to Heaven, to show that dying while in sin such as unforgiveness or adultery can lead you to hell unless you repent sincerely as you’re alive. God has shown people these things and brought them back to life on assignment to teach the world that not everyone will have the luxury of deathbed repentance.

These are the deeper things of God that many do not want to hear let alone believe. The idea of believing in Christ and drawing the line there, thinking Heaven is your home no matter what, is too convenient for these end times. The Word tells us we will face greater persecution today than in the days of Paul. How strong would God's army of people be in the end times if everyone was saved regardless of what they chose, if only for the fact that they read

Jesus was the Christ and believed it on the surface? That's no different than placing oversized armor on a small child and calling them a seasoned veteran soldier.

Many people will refuse to believe this simple fact. Truthfully, even those that remain who acknowledge this fact may not be making Heaven their home. The Word tells us in Matthew 7:21-23 (NIV) "Not everyone who says to me, 'Lord, Lord,' will enter the kingdom of heaven, but only he who does the will of my father who is in heaven. Many will say to me on that day, 'Lord, Lord, did we not prophesy in your name, and in your name drive out demons and perform many miracles?' Then I will tell them plainly, 'I never knew you. Away from me, you evildoers!"

Yes, this means Christians and believers who know the Word of God, who use the authority and power of Christ given them, to cast out demons and heal the sick, to prophesy and speak in tongues, those who claim to know Jesus and profess He is Lord, yet if they die in unrepentant sin will find themselves rejected from Heaven by the Lord Himself. If this doesn't wake you up to the reality that your salvation must be worked out each day, then there is a spirit from hell assigned to block the truth of the Word from entering your spirit, and you need a deliverance from the demonic realm that you have allowed to gain a foothold in your life, and establish strongholds within your temple because of sins you have committed, or even generational curses that have been left unbroken.

The truth is, if you are truly sold out to God and are willing to pick up your cross and follow Him, then you will hear and know God's voice and His heart. You should be able to know where you stand with God, and if He is angry with you or well pleased with you. This can only be done as you walk in the spirit and not the flesh. The flesh is worldly and subject to confusion and destruction. The spirit is where God does the ministering and where the truth of the Word abides. You can only achieve walking in the spirit by dying to your flesh. The Word tells us to crucify our flesh! Put God first. Put God first in your heart – love Him the most, even more than your wife or husband. Love God more than your own children. Absolutely anything you place before God is an idol. This can be a desire, a thought, a person, an object, and a game, anything that you put before God.

I have seen men of God who place God totally first that they could even rejoice in the midst of the death of their spouse, simply because they know God is able to keep them and they know their spouse is in Heavenly places rejoicing with them. By loving God more than everything else, the enemy could not steal from them to the point it would destroy them. When you make God your mainstay and your solid rock, you won't be as hurt when you lose anything else. This is a blessing of a close and intimate walk with God.

In my short time I have seen people who have sat under a highly anointed church and prophet/pastor, hearing the Word of God for over 30 years – but refusing to change from their ways of sin. God has shown longsuffering and patience and has even given grace at the very last breath of people's lives... but in these end times, there's no more time for games and no more room for play. Many will fall away as chaff and weeds to be burned in the fire. Jesus spoke in parables and gave us insight to what the end times would look like – and it is surely here right now.

Many people do not heed the cry for repentance. Many people refuse to believe God can cut his grace in half, let alone completely. Many still deny that God will judge America for her wicked sins. But I tell you that God will surely send judgment upon the United States for her harlotry and it's blackest of sin. Truthfully, God is angry at America and the gavel has already struck down in the courtroom of Heaven. The sins of Babylon (America) have reached the throne room of Heaven and God has decreed that it must be judged once and for all. I tell you that you will not recognize this nation when the Most High is finished with it. These are words of condemnation that will be met with much criticism and hatred, but there is still hope for the remnant of those who choose to follow Christ at all costs, wholeheartedly.

Countless times God has shown me visions and dreams of the destruction of California and other states, showing the judgment that will be poured out upon the Earth itself. I have seen horrible situations of poverty, rioting, looting, pillaging, plague, famine, drought, solar flares that torched skin, meteors that slammed into the Earth, corpses and deaths of men, women and children. It is not because God is uncaring or full of hate – it is a warning that the enemy will soon have his rule and reign over this world, and those hardened and unrepentant hearts will be subject to Satan's judgment along with all the demonic realm and fallen angels.

Rather God is full of Grace, by showing these things to His prophets and seers before they happen, so the world may have a chance to hear the Word of Truth and repent. But the message of hope is this: God will keep His own; He will supply and sustain His true children who abide in Him, the Almighty One.

God spoke to me in one of my first prophetic words and told me the plan for my life and what I would be doing. God did this even at a time that I may not have fully understood at all... but He gave me hope at a time that I needed encouragement. In that Word, God told me that I would carry His truth to the nations, even to the dignitaries of the land,

and proclaim His Truth and to tell the leaders of the nation how to avoid the coming disasters that would fall upon America. However, God warned me that because I bring news of destruction and suffering, that many people would come against me and not heed the words God speaks through me.

In my second assignment, I experienced resistance to the words I spoke as I ministered to this person who at that present time was struggling with drug addictions. We need to understand how God and His Holy Spirit work before we can minister to people. We must understand that it takes the Holy Spirit to be able to reach into someone's heart and save them. As humans, we may be able to sway people or cause them to think and feel certain ways with emotions and the like, but only God can save a soul. It is our duty to plant the seed and move on, unless God specifically tells you to work with watering the seed and charging you with its development into completion.

God had given a word over this person I was assigned to, and God knew the path this person would ultimately choose and what would happen thereafter. I was an instrument to be used in this person's life to help them return to Christ completely and show them that God can supernaturally heal a person who was deeply into drugs, without withdrawals. Such a thing could give hope to one in that situation. This was grace that God showed to me and allowed me an opportunity to shine His light into another person's situation.

The prideful will never make it, and the haughty cannot serve God. On both of my assignments, I was made low before men and God. I was placed in circumstances to teach me how to be a servant. As a hard headed and stubborn person myself, it has taken a lot of longsuffering and patience for the blessed souls to deal with me – but God prevailed and so did they. If we are not willing to take the servants towel over our arm here on Earth, and serve others, then we will never be as Christ has asked us to be; therefore neglecting the laws of God and forfeiting our rightful places in Heaven.

There are many parts to Heaven and the coming age, those who worked all their lives for Christ and sacrificing the things of this world while storing their treasures up in Heaven – Jesus has prepared a place for them according to the works of their life on Earth. Those who lived a life of sin and experienced repentance on their deathbed may still make it into Heaven, but if only to sweep the streets with a golden broom.

What does it mean to serve others on this Earth? It means to allow God to use you, and place you into circumstances and situations where you may even suffer, for the purpose of allowing God to minister to a soul that He has chosen to minister to –

through you. Look back at my first assignment and you will see how important a single soul is to God.

Throughout the duration of my second assignment, many things transpired in my life. I was prophesied that I would have a new home, a new vehicle, and even a wife – all in the year 2012. This was prophesied to me in February of 2012. The things that unfolded came to pass exactly as God said they would. And here we encounter where God's promises are intended and designed for our best interests, however our own free will and choice can affect God's perfect plan – which is why we should take very seriously the consequences of our actions especially knowing that we will all one day be held accountable for our actions, thoughts and feelings. God promised me that the move from my extended family's house to the next place would be my own home. However, that did not come to pass because the person I was first assigned to did not pass the test God had designed. Remember that God does not go against a person's free will, and at this point God had to recalculate my spiritual GPS route.

Humble hearts that are submitted to God's will shall always be able to adapt to God's plans and live with the joy of the Lord deep in their hearts. Even when they feel hopeless, they can draw on the joy of the Lord to carry them through their darkest hour. God has given me a scripture for those who are hopeless and destitute – which can be found in Isaiah

22:13 (NIV) "But see, there is joy and revelry, slaughtering of cattle and killing of sheep, eating of meat and drinking of wine! 'Let us eat and drink,' you say, 'for tomorrow we die!'" It is explained that these people said amongst themselves to feast and drink, because they gave up on hope. In this chapter, these people were being attacked on all sides and chose hopelessness. Two common choices appear when faced with hopelessness – despair and self-indulgence. But God promises eternal life to those that follow, so there should be no acting as though all hope is lost, because this world is not the end of all things. This is a powerful scripture that can be applied to how nations will respond to God's judgment, and create an opportunity of revival proportions to show that there is hope in the Lord Jesus Christ.

One thing that God has taught me since I started in 2012 seeking diligently after Him, was that we do not understand all things. There is so much more to this world and the way things work behind the scenes. The spiritual realm is far larger than anyone could imagine. The war that takes place around us is great and will soon become so immense and critical; it will actually begin to manifest itself in the natural in the final days.

I have witnessed spirits of deception and mind control intercept the word of God, and twist it as it goes through a person's mind and prevent that word from taking root in their spirit. The words of truth that God speaks never reach that persons heart where it can take root and grow, leading to the manifestation of a Godly lifestyle. Jesus tells us of the parable of the four soils in Matthew 13. There are spiritual forces of wickedness working diligently to bind and hinder you, and those around you. Many people do not believe in deliverance or in deliverance ministries. For those that believe the full word of God you will see that Jesus sends us forth into the world as He was sent forth (John 20:21 NIV) and to do the works as He did them (John 14:12 NIV) and also gives us authority to do the works at hand (Mark 13:34 NIV)

With these facts being established, we begin to see more of the truth and ask ourselves why demons would possess people. They work for the kingdom of darkness and they exist to steal, kill and destroy. They hate God because He judged them and lifted His grace from them. Now, because we are made in the image of God, and because we are God's most prized creation, they strike against God by targeting us. They exist to keep you away from God, causing eternal separation from God as you are judged and sent to the lake of fire as well, for not receiving his redemptive grace in His Son Jesus Christ. God does not wash his hands of your existence even if you were condemned to hell… The Lord Jesus walks through hell and weeps over the souls who never received Him. But none can say they never had a chance, never had an opportunity, or never had hope. God constantly tries to reach out to us the entire duration of our lives, yet being possessed and oppressed by demons can hinder and distort the voice of God and the call of God for us to come into His kingdom. It is up to you right now to make a conscious decision to open your ears sincerely to the leading of God and the voice of God. It is up to you right now to choose you want to hear God's plan for your life, to leave your heart and mind open to receive what He has for you. You must have faith and believe that God is real and loves you, and can reach out to you in any way shape or form; for nothing is impossible with God. Just as God does not go against your free will, the enemy also cannot go against your spoken word. Decree a thing in the name of Jesus, with sincerity of heart and faith... and you have created a weapon the enemy cannot break.

I am constantly in warfare, praying and decreeing against the enemy. Each time I write in this book, the enemy attacks me and uses those closest to me. It has taken the hand of God to give me grace to be in a place where I can complete it. God has called me and chosen me to save a million souls, and the enemy will stop at nothing to use anyone or anything to come against me to quit doing what God has asked me to do. But the Holy Spirit within me shall prevail, and has prevailed. Do not sit by idly and allow the enemy to steal from you or discourage you. Use the weapons of warfare God has given you, the full armor of God, and the Word of God, to fight the spiritual battle taking place around you. Paul spoke of these weapons and the tools God has given us. But what do they profit us if we do not understand how to use them? The enemy laughs at the armor of God, if it is simply left hanging up on a shelf unused. But equip them, and wield them mightily with faith and boldness, and the enemy will flee.

Chapter 8: The Third Assignment

At this point I was holding on to many promises from God, but had yet to learn the lesson that disobedience is one of the many sins that hinders God from bringing forth what He desires to give us.

In my case, God has blessed me with an abundance of grace. He could have washed His hands of me long ago, but still chose to continue to woo me to do His works and at last it has gotten through to my heart to do the works God has called me to do. Many roads I have gone down to learn this lesson, and each time the road became more difficult when I refused to yield. The final road was that my blessings and the blessings of those around me were in jeopardy. This is what finally caught my attention, as my salvation was at stake depending on whether or not I yielded to God's Will.

One night during a deliverance session, I was assisting others in the casting out of spirits that God was revealing to us. As we worked on this person, I saw a vision in the spirit realm. It was a woman who was attending our church on Wednesday evenings, I saw her face clearly and her lips moved in sync with the words I heard spoken from her. It was very detailed and real. I saw her on her knees, praying to the Lord as she said, "Give him a sign that I do feel the same way about him as he feels about me." This vision was so powerful it distracted me from focusing on the deliverance, and I stepped aside at the next opportunity to talk to my pastor and ask what this meant. I was uncertain if this was from God or the enemy, because it happened at a time I did not expect. But it was from God, and I stepped out in faith according to what God had shown me.

I had an affinity for this woman but had never talked with her. She had six children but lived in a broken home. I was fond of her children in church, something about them always stuck out with me and they all had a special place in my heart. In the past I had ministered and taught this group of children in the ways of the Lord, and used my past as an example to illustrate the power and purpose of the enemy, his tactics and plans to steal, kill and destroy.

After receiving this vision from God about her, the next church service I approached her and rather nervously (but in faith) explained the vision I received without going into vivid detail… I was only comfortable to say to her that I share what she feels. She was floored that I had said that, because she felt a similar way about me. We exchanged letters as we met each other at church, talking about ourselves and getting to know each other. We had a very strong spiritual connection and developed a friendship as time went on. God would tell me that she and I were meant to be together, and that she was my soul mate. God had previously asked me to leave my previous relationship, and I did not understand why at the time, but I did it in obedience. When God spoke this recent relationship over me, I understood why.

One time I talked with my pastor, and I vented my frustration to her that it seems like God has always kept me away from women or that my relationships have failed quickly or tragically, and it seemed like I was never allowed to have one. The Spirit of God fell upon that room and she prophesied as God simply spoke to me and said, "That is the one thing I have kept from you."

God spoke with such power, that my frustration and confusion fled immediately. Many years of pain and sorrow with uncertainty was washed away and healed with a simple Word from God. I believed that since God had it under control then everything will be okay and there is nothing to worry about.

I would soon marry this woman and become part of her blended family, which was a prayer of many years that would finally be answered. As I was a child, I always admired the strong marriage my parents had and how stable they were together. That was my model framework to use to rely on and build upon for my own relationship – and now I finally had one to work with. It was interesting to see God's humor, and also His blessings. I have always wanted a girl as my first child, and here now God blessed me with seven girls altogether.

God had desired for us to walk out our friendship and relationship at a certain pace. Many times we were chastised for going too fast; because God was doing a works in people around us. It was very critical and important to follow God's timing in our relationship because it was more than just about us. We never see the full scope of the work God is doing in people around us, and we do not understand with our limited capacity how God works. The Word of God tells us in Isaiah 55:8-9 (NIV): "'For my thoughts are not your thoughts, neither are your ways my ways,' declares the Lord. 'As the heavens are higher than the earth, so are my ways higher than your ways and my thoughts than your thoughts.'"

God once gave me a very encouraging word, and He told me that I was surely His and that there were two things that made me very special and unique in the Kingdom of God: A higher walk, and a deeper calling. There is much joy, and many benefits to be reaped from this, yet it also carries a heavy cost. God is very strict with me and when I am out of His Will, He will chastise me severely. The way God speaks to me may not be the same He speaks to another person, or even you. God knows me because He created me, and He knows how to penetrate the thickness of my head. My hardheadedness may be a personality trait that God can use, as long as I am hard headed FOR God and not against Him. If you can apply the firmness and unmoving devotion to God's ways rather than your own ways, you can succeed in being so steadfast, sure, steady and bold for God that no one and nothing could convince you otherwise.

I found myself in this marriage having this responsibility, and working with a diverse multitude of children. At first I was afraid, because I myself am still young at only 28 years of age, and I had heard of horror stories of stepping into a family's life as a step parent. My children are currently aged 15, 14, 14, 10, 8 and 2. They are all girls. As I said, God has a sense of humor and knows how to answer prayers in abundance. I knew this was all called of God because this family accepted me immediately without hesitation, even despite their circumstances in the past. Two of them called me dad even before I married their mother, and we only knew each other for about 6 months before our marriage. God had told me months before that our marriage was secure and it was going to happen.

I have cried many nights because of God's power and authority; He who has all authority over every situation in our lives. God is sovereign and in control. I asked God for a sign to show me that He is securing our marriage and that if He did, I would dance as David danced. One night in the back yard on a cold and starry night, I was outside praying. I contended with God, and reminded Him that He once told me that He has moved Heaven and Earth on my behalf. Then I asked Him to move the universe, to show me two shooting stars in a row. I asked for something specific and unlikely, to be sure it is of God. Lo and behold, after 2 minutes, I saw exactly what I prayed. I beheld two shooting stars, in the *same exact place*. This was something even more unlikely than I asked for – this was God showing His power and answering my prayer. He is more powerful even than my imagination could muster. I then danced for God, as David danced, without hindrance or regret. Dancing is something I refuse to do in the natural, and I dislike it intensely. But for God, I gave Him the pleasure of watching me in pure joy.

The following is a prophetic word from God:

"My children, who will heed Me? Who will come before Me in repentance? Who will be made mighty in My army? For I am the great I Am. Behold, as I reach out to the multitudes, so few answer My call. The kingdom of darkness will rule and reign for a season, and so many will fall away and be cast out of my presence. It will take the secure heart that is grounded in My Son, to be able to withstand the power of darkness that shall come over the land. Who shall come into My land and yield all to Me? I have promised you eternal life, I have already given the sacrifice and paid the price for you. All you need do is step up and receive My Son, and follow Me."

The Spirit of God is upon you and brings forth conviction, which leads to repentance, which opens you to receive the things of God. Do not fight the leading of the Holy Spirit; it is He that will guide you to God the Father, through Christ Jesus.

The problem with churches today is that most of them don't truly serve God at all. The world attempts to seek Christ within the church and only finds more of the world. How is this winning anyone to Christ? Just this evening I was in line at the register of a store, I had a small basket of dinner items we needed as I was waiting near the register with my daughter. I turned to ask the people behind me if they wanted to go before me, because they had more items than I did. They politely declined, and so I turned my attention to the woman in front of me several moments later. Her total was slightly over forty dollars. She had two twenties but nothing else. She had to run out to her car to get extra change. Before I could catch her, she was already out the door – but I asked the cashier how much extra she owed, and I paid the difference for her. When the woman returned to the register, I simply handed her back the change I received. I explained that it was paid for her and she seemed astonished. She was very persistent in asking me to receive the money back that I paid, and I agreed only because I didn't want to offend her. I used the opportunity to illustrate the love of Christ, and I told her to have a blessed evening. As I paid for my things, and left the store I met the woman outside in the parking lot. She thanked me again and I could see the happiness in her eyes. I prayed that God would touch her and use this act to be able to reach through to her and I prayed to release the angels to go forth and minister to her.

By every action you commit, you open doors or close doors. These things affect your life and the lives of the people around you. Negative behavior can shut doors for yourself and close opportunities for people around you as well. Acts of righteousness could open doors for flagrant sinners to lead them to Christ, and many other possibilities. The word of God says that love prevails. This is why God calls us to love the unlovable. Your work may seem to have no effect, but it is through your work, that God can move upon a person's heart no matter how hardened it might be. It is true that some people are destined to never serve God, but the grace and opportunities are always there – and therefore no man has any excuse of why they did not serve God.

As I wrote the above paragraph, God spoke to me and said to read 1 John 2:19 (NIV) "They went out from us, but they did not really belong to us. For if they had belonged to us, they would have remained with us; but their going showed that none of them belonged to us." I believe God is showing us that there are people who seem to be very Christ-like, but actually have the Antichrist spirit at work within them, perhaps never yielding to God. If you watch the fruit that people bare, you will know by which spirit they obey. This is why it is so important to be living in the Spirit and praying unceasingly for discernment from Heaven. God can allow you to see through a person into their heart and allow you to see as He sees them. Through the eyes of Christ, you will see the truth.

God has me on my third assignment, which is to be a light in a dark place. God foretold of this at the beginning of January 2012, and here it has come to pass even in November of 2012. My assignment is to die to my flesh and live by the spirit, so that the Holy Spirit can abide in me thoroughly and completely, therefore His presence and light can radiate out of my vessel to touch the souls of those around me. My children have come from a very colorful background; many of them were so disheveled and programmed with negative outlooks. They were shown that the idea of a father was an abusive and neglectful figure. Their idea of a man was someone who serves himself and comes and goes as he pleases, someone who's only worth and value is to work at a job and bring money home and that's as far as their responsibility goes. They have seen women treated as though they are inferior and there was at one point in time a deeply rooted resentment for males in their psyche. Marrying into this blended family with this type of background has presented its own challenges, but by the grace of God they have all received me with open arms. I truly believe that it is the spirit of God working through me that they have received with open arms. All I have done is made a willing choice to serve God and be used by Him at all cost, and the rest God has done and it is His honor and glory and He gets all the credit.

My wife and I teach our girls by example as well as with our words, that husband and wife are equal and share responsibility together to raise children in God's ways. We make decisions together, we constantly stay by each other's sides, and even when we have family meetings or disciplinary situations, my wife and I are together holding hands the entire time to illustrate the power of our unity and conformity with each other. Our kids could ask mom or dad a question in separate rooms and get the same answer out of both of us – our unity and agreement is solid. This has provided a feeling of stability for our children. They never need to worry anymore about disunity or arguments flying around the household when it comes to mom and dad. They see that we are stable in our choices and we illustrate that it's unacceptable to undermine authority.

I must illustrate that this paragraph focuses on me as a dad, from a man's perspective. My wife and I share equal responsibility and we raise our children together all the same – but I would like to try and reach out to fathers and dads with this area. I talk with my children, as a dad, and I show them that I do care about them by listening to them. Sometimes our kids just need us to listen while we hold our tongues and quit trying to correct them at every single solitary turn. I am not saying to ignore discipline when it is needed, but you must be careful to discern when to correct and when to simply listen. This builds confidence in them towards you. As a dad, I sometimes spend time with them doing the things that they like and prefer to do. One night I sat down and painted the nails of my wife and daughters as a family time event. We talked and laughed, and believe me most of the laughing was directed toward me, but we all had a great time and I showed them that as a dad, I can participate in the things they like and not just what I want. This has built a loving, father-daughter relationship with my children. When it comes to discipline, as a step-dad, (though I do not like to use those titles, I believe that being placed here to care for them and raise them earns the title of dad) I am quick to correct an issue, although each child needs different presentations and forms of discipline, it is all done by grace and in love. This is the important key most dads are missing. You need love and grace combined with purity and discipline. Knowing when to be stern and unmoving and when to be lenient and accommodating to their needs (but never compromising) is paramount. It takes wisdom and discernment beyond my years to raise them and this knowledge has been provided by God.

You need to be careful not to become your child's best friend. Leave that title to others their age that they can better relate to. Your job as a dad is to be strictly a dad. The reason is most parents who treat their children as best friends have actually caused their children to lose the ability to learn from their mistakes after you correct them. This can cause other issues and side effects with how they themselves will be a parent, or how they will handle themselves later in life. My children can come and talk to me if they desire to, but I will not keep secrets from my wife and I will inform her of everything so that we know how to pray together in unity for our children. The benefits of a solid and stable Christian marriage is that we can share everything without causing problems, and the result is always to gain insight on how to improve our circumstances or how to protect each other through prayer. You can interact with your children as a dad without being their best friend. Too many people think they have to be the child's best friend to do things with them and that is not the case.

I find myself in a place that by doing God's will there is a lot of responsibility on my shoulders. It was easy beforehand to attempt God's tasks by myself with no hindrance and plenty of free time throughout the day. As of now, I am married with 6 children and it is difficult to find time to accomplish what God has asked me to do – but many things depend on me completing my task. We have been promised a new home and a new vehicle, and our current situation is critical. God has told me that the task He has given me is so important, that this book and these warfare songs must be written, published and recorded or else I won't stand a chance to make Heaven my home. Not only that, but if I fail in my assignment here then my wife and children will not have a new home waiting for them.

We are currently here in this place enduring an extreme and radical environment straight from the pits of hell. God placed us here (and this thorn in our flesh) for two purposes. We must learn to praise God during the storm, and live as humble servants even towards a "Pharaoh" personality. Secondly, this soul that we were sent to has a last chance to experience the Grace of God and turn from their wicked ways and be redeemed. God uses us as the vessels to undergo this harsh task and be subjected to different levels of torment because we are willing and have once said, "Here I am Lord, use me."

God is not enjoying our suffrage; He is simply using a person to pass His love through to a lost soul who is dying. At a time that God sees fit, He will determine the ultimate state of that soul and make a judgment and move us forward. Does it sound cruel to you? If God would sacrifice His own Son, and allow Him to be subjected to the worst of torment, to redeem all of mankind – wouldn't it stand to reason that if you love the Lord and pick up your cross and follow Him, that you would be subject to persecution and being placed in uncomfortable positions for the sake of another? In all things God does, love is the root of it. Follow the love, and you will find the reason.

I am learning that 9 people can suffer unimaginably all for the sake of 1 soul. This assignment I have been given is to allow God to use me and my family to attempt to bring 1 soul back to His kingdom. By showing nothing but love, despite being hated and despised each day, despite our children going through constant torment, we must obey in love. God is a righteous and just God. He will explore every possible avenue; He will give every possible chance, so that in the end there will be absolutely no excuses and no arguments. In the end, God has given every grace and every opportunity to each soul. If you did not make it into His kingdom, there will be no pleading your case. The judgment has been set. And how terrible it will be on that day for those who must live eternally in torment, remembering every chance they had but did not take for one selfish reason or another.

God has us walk in His ways, to keep us safe from the enemy. This is a learning process. Some people can be touched by God supernaturally and change overnight. But oftentimes people who are delivered or changed instantly may struggle holding onto their newness in Christ. In my experience, those who must go through long trials and endure much painstaking refinery typically hold onto their new habits in Christ more firmly and tend not to backslide. We must look forward to the understanding of doing things God's way and watching to see the benefits and peace we attain by doing this. And it is not easy by any measure... the flesh and the mind wants to dictate our actions many times during pressure and stress, but you will learn how to seek God first for all things and pray before each situation.

There are many times when I desire to handle things in my own ways or respond to a situation in my flesh especially when it comes to our children; but because of what God has told me, I must take great care in how I treat them. God already told me once never to beset them, that I must give order, stability and discipline in their lives but that I must always show them grace and love. The most important thing to give them is love, above all else. There is much discipline in love, as the word of God tells us that a person who loves their children will chastise them and use the rod of discipline. While I do not use a rod to strike my children, I can be stern and unmoving with the truth to cause them to think about their actions and behaviors.

Over the months of having been married and living with my new family, I have seen many awesome changes taking place in everyone's lives. I have noticed that as I allowed God's light to operate and shine through me, two things have occurred. The light inside of people's hearts has become much brighter and the darkness in hearts has gotten even darker. The presence of God has this effect on people around you, and this brings forth the fruits of the heart to the surface for you to see the truth. When confronted with the light of God, the darkness in people will manifest itself. At that time, it must be recognized and dealt with. The person who is bound with spirits must admit and accept that they are bound and have these issues. They must be willing to accept deliverance, or else no spirit will leave because they have a legal right due to that persons doubt and unbelief. If God is dealing with a person by Himself, then His sovereignty and perfect will can deliver people by His own accord.

It is true that we must love one another and never hold ought towards a brother or sister in Christ. The bible tells us in 1 John 2:9-11 (NIV) "Anyone who claims to be in the light but hates his brother is still in the darkness. Whoever loves his brother lives in the light, and there is nothing in him to make him stumble. But whoever hates his brother is in the darkness and walks around in the darkness; he does not know where he is going, because the darkness has blinded him." This does not mean that if we dislike someone we're not Christians. The bible teaches us that it is okay to be angry, but it clearly commands us not to sin in our anger. This passage is telling us not to treat others in a way that would cause us to neglect them or despise them, or to treat them as irritants. It is our choice to treat others with respect and concern ourselves with their wellbeing as humans, rather than focusing on their actions or sins and judging them for ourselves.

I have made mistakes along the way, but God has always corrected me and warned me. God has sometimes spoken to me in the most strict and stern way that I felt as though I would die the next night in my sleep from His anger. But I was brought out of a place from being distraught, because God told me that He disciplines and chastises those He loves and that if He did not love me, He would let me go about my ways without warning. This is the very same with our children. Some parents are too scared to discipline their children, out of fear of what they might think or feel towards them. But love includes discipline with it, sometimes even tough love, strictness and those tough choices. When done properly, these things will show your children that you love them and they will know and understand that love. Some children take longer to learn than others, and some must go down harder roads than others, but they will eventually understand all you did out of love and how it brings them to where they need to be; this is the very same way with God.

A free-for-all parent is one who mostly allows a child to do or have what they want and maintains the 'best friend' relationship with them. Unfortunately, for whatever reason a parent chooses to follow this path, whether for ease of parenting or out of fear, the consequences result in leaving your child starving for motherly or fatherly attention and love. But they never really do find it – and they look in all the wrong places. In many cases these types of children find themselves in abusive relationships and end up being dominated by evil.

When is the last time you set limits on your children? God sets limits on us. When is the last time you encouraged your child and taught them how to raise their standards and expectations? God constantly encourages us rather than belittles us for our current state.

The Lord had taken me from a place where I was alone and had very few responsibilities. I was used to handling things my own way, with my own method of thinking, and my own style. I didn't have people around me to cause me to check or analyze my own ways to consider if they were truly effective or if they were destructive. But the Lord knew my heart, even when I did not. Even through all my sin and transgressions, God pardoned me with His favor and mercy and even answered my greatest prayer of 15 years. Now here I stand, having come from a solitary life, being the youngest of my family – to being a dad to 6 girls, and a husband to an amazing woman whom God Himself said is my soul mate even in the new Earth and the end of the age. It is only by the wisdom and grace of God that I am able to transition from my past life into the new one God has set before me, where I must now consider other people's feelings and points of view. I must humble myself and submit to the circumstances around me to stay pure and work through God's will and not my own. These changes are drastic ones, but necessary to the fulfillment of God's purposes in my life. It is mercy and grace from God that has made this possible.

Chapter 9: America

The great nation of America finds itself standing before the judgment seat of Christ. This nation has been declining spiritually for decades, and it is full of all manners of sin and perversion. The fact that this nation is removing God from its roots is only a very small part of it, hardly comparable to the gross darkness that pervades this nation's borders with such mass and density. There is a super stronghold of Antichrist hovering over this nation. The very heart of hell pumps the blackened blood of sin through the veins of America. If you do not believe it, then read Romans 1:18 (NIV) "The wrath of God is being revealed from heaven against all the godlessness and wickedness of men who suppress the truth by their wickedness ... " and it goes on to list envy, murder, strife, deceit, malice, gossip, slander, God-haters, insolence, arrogance, boastfulness, inventing ways of doing evil, disobeying parents, senselessness, faithlessness, heartlessness and ruthlessness as manners of wickedness that are all deserving of death, because the people have known God's righteous decree yet ignore it and even approve of those who practice them.

How long will God be patient, longsuffering and merciful to mankind in these depths of sin we see all around us, constantly? How long will God allow people to trample on the blood of His son Jesus Christ? The blood of Jesus is crying out for revenge, because this nation has abandoned God through almost every avenue of its operation and lifestyle.

The Word tells us that the wrath of God is being revealed from Heaven. And the truth is that what may be known about God has been made plain to man, because God made it plain to man. There is absolutely no excuse for not knowing and understanding right from wrong, according to the one and only true God. God's invisible qualities have been clearly seen from the beginning. There is absolutely no excuse to give to God for why you did not know Him or serve Him. Romans 1:25 (NIV) says, "They exchanged the truth of God for a lie, and worshiped and served created things rather than the Creator – who is forever praised. Amen." In today's society, the people tend to believe lies that reinforce or promote their own negative or selfish beliefs and behaviors. Today, we must be careful of input from Television, movies, music and other forms of media including the Internet – that presents sinful lifestyles and unwholesome values. We are literally plagued by ideals, attitudes and beliefs that are opposed to the bible. We must be careful of what we allow to form our opinions. The bible itself is the only standard of truth we have for reference in this world, and you would do well and be wise to compare all opinions to the bible.

Would Jesus watch that TV show? Does the bible approve of that persons behavior? Are your thoughts the same type of thoughts God would have? Do you look at the heart in mercy, or do you look at the flesh in judgment?

God is angry at the church in America. The church has forsaken God and pleasured itself in sin. They teach only partial bits of the truth, withholding others and omitting facts. In these times pastors are being arrested for preaching parts of the bible here in churches in America. Many churches preach once-saved-always-saved doctrine and falsehoods. Too many churches preach outright lies straight from the depths of hell – and all these souls are lost and dying. The people are self-deceived and they believe they are going to heaven, but what a terrible fate to be judged by God only to be sentenced to hell for unrepentant sin. Many churches do not teach about the sensitive and controversial issue of homosexuality, out of fear of being arrested. Because the church has a spirit of fear operating within it, a stronghold is established which has opened the door for false doctrine and deception to operate securely within the congregation. The house of God has now become the synagogue of Satan. The house of God should teach the Word of God in its fullness, teaching by the leading of the Holy Spirit to be in truth and in spirit. The leaders will be judged even more harshly because they are accountable for the flock placed under their guidance.

It is important to see that God can literally hand you over to the enemy. This fact is proven in Romans chapter 1 and also chapter 2:26, and 2:28. Because of the hardened and unrepentant hearts of the people, God handed them over to shameful lusts and depraved minds. Look in the book of Exodus and read about Pharaoh. God hardened his heart, and God knew even when he created Pharaoh, that he would never live to serve Him. But that didn't stop God from giving him fair grace and opportunity. But this fact remains that some people are born destined for hell. These types of people are born of a different spirit than the spirit of God. The spirit realm holds so much, is so deep and complex – only God's wisdom can reveal these things.

America must snap out of its self-deceived state and repent! But we live in a time where repentance will not stop the judgment that is coming forth. This nation has become worse than Sodom and Gomorrah, and this was spoken by God. I have seen many visions of what is to come upon this nation and the destruction is pure shock and awe. Many woes are going to be poured out over the land in great abundance. It will seem like there is no rest at all, and so many people will fall into the darkness.

The church won't suffice any longer. All religion has been decreed as dead fruit by the Most High God. The word of God is not working anymore to reach into the hearts of the people. Now it is only spirit calling unto spirit; and only by the leading of the Holy Spirit will you be able to make it in these end times. You must learn now to rely on the Holy Spirit's guidance. You must learn right now, how to discern between God's Holy Spirit and the false spirit of the Antichrist. If you are bound and demon possessed, which most people are, including born again Christians – then you are being hindered and shall be hindered greater still in the coming days of darkness that will come across the land. God is telling His prophets and His chosen people what is going to happen before it ever happens. He is even revealing great mysteries in the Heavens and explaining what is taking place in the spirit realm.

Those who judge others are only judging themselves, because they themselves have done the same things in their hearts that they accuse others of doing. Let us read Romans 2:4 (NIV) "Or do you show contempt for the riches of his kindness, tolerance and patience, not realizing that God's kindness leads you toward repentance?" God has held back His judgment, giving the people of this nation time to repent. However, the people have been mistaking God's patience for the approval of their wrongdoing and their sinful lifestyles. Self-evaluation is very difficult in these days where reflecting on your own actions is seldom taught or appreciated in a society of greed, selfishness, being served and having instant gratification. Sadly, we are more amazed at God's patience with others rather than being humbled at His patience with us.

It's part of God's nature to be long-suffering and enduring, striving to cultivate Godliness in His chosen vessels – but will they listen? Will they heed the call before it is too late? God calls to us until our last breath, but now we live in the end times and the season for preparation is behind us because it is time to fight right now. It is time to answer right now. Those who do not answer right now will be left behind altogether, and they will do without.

John 12:48 (NIV) says, “There is a judge for the one who rejects me and does not accept my words; that very word which I spoke will condemn him at the last day.” Those who listened to Jesus Christ and lived His way will be raised to eternal life, yet those who rejected even some of His words will be condemned for those that they refused to live by. They will be judged according to every deed, good or evil. Ecclesiastes 12:14 (NIV) says, “For God will bring every deed into judgment, including every hidden thing, whether it is good or evil.”

America must wake up and realize that it is being punished by God, and that it deserves to be punished, and that there is nothing that can be done to pray it away. The cost of sin has added up and has been calculated. The scales have been set fairly and accurately, they have been tested and weighed – and the heart of America has been weighed against the standard of the Holy Living God. America has been found guilty of abominations against the Spirit of God, and she refuses to repent.

What hope then is there for this nation? The prophets have dreams and visions and hear the voice of God speaking against this nation, yet the ears of its people refuse to listen. In their self-deception, their hearts are hardened and they do not allow themselves the opportunity to repent. When the woes come, and judgment falls upon them, they will not cry out to God and repent begging for mercy. They will curse God and fall away from him, because they have been handed over to the enemy. They have walked crooked paths and lived falsely, walking in deception and manipulating one another. They have served themselves on the inside while appearing to serve others on the outside. Even their genuine service to others has ulterior motives and secret desires. Such a heart cannot give without expectation of return; they give begrudgingly in their hearts and such is the root of unforgiveness that has taken them into captivity in hell. While all these things have taken place in their lives they never noticed it, because the enemy came to them as a wolf in sheep's clothing; like a thief in the night he stole from them and left them naked and ashamed, weeping and wailing in the midst of gnashing teeth.

Are you hearing but not understanding? Will you have the humility to be humbled and evaluate yourself? This is sacred to maintaining your walk with God each day. If you have heard the word of the Lord through His prophets, then you must test the fruit of that Word. A true prophet of God will minister the Word in Truth and in Spirit, with each prophetic statement that comes from God there is a message of instruction, and a message of hope. Where there is love, there is hope. And because God IS love; by proxy there is hope in God. The only way you have been deemed hopeless is by your own decision to harden your heart. You allowed the enemy to come in and bring with him doubt and unbelief, and because you believed his lies you are now in bondage. The answer to all hopelessness is true repentance. You must tear down the walls around your heart and accept that you might actually not be all that and then some. You must allow the Holy Spirit to convict you and minister to you any wrongs you might have done that were not pleasing to God. Then you must accept this fact and repent truthfully, with sincerity, and then move on. You don't need to dwell on the fact you sinned or have gone astray, because guilt and condemnation are not from God, but from Satan. The enemy tries to remind you of all your past failures and shortcomings to deter you and distract you from following God. When the enemy does this, just remind him of his future.

What is happening is the end times are here, now. These are the very beginnings, the precursor to the events that have been foretold in the Bible. Church is done. Religion is done. It is strictly about the Spirit of God calling to the spirit in you. I say that "church" and "religion" are done, because these facets of faith are failing and have been corrupted. Why won't church and religion work in these times? It is because the leaders of the church live in sin and preach false doctrine. It is because the people do not receive the full truth due to their desire to continue in unrepentant sin. It is because the blind are leading the blind; and they both fall into a ditch. They will not yield to the Spirit of God. Many don't believe in prophets, many don't believe in deliverance. Many say Christians can't have demons in them, many teach that some sins are actually okay. Many are afraid to preach the truth because it could land them in prison. Many churches and pastors and other ministers of the gospel teach that God is too good to punish people. Too many television evangelists preach a "name it and claim it" message, stating that you have every right to prosper financially because Jesus died for all your sins. No... Jesus died for your sins so that you would not be automatically condemned to hell, period. The blessings are given to you only by the choice and grace of God, assuming you follow Him completely with all your mind, heart, body and soul. Assuming you have crucified your flesh, and desire only the will of the Father, practicing every good fruit of the Spirit in your daily life; in which case you would not be begging for money in prayer, but only that God's perfect will be done in your life. As you live in the Spirit, you shall pray in the Spirit, and by doing this you will always pray the will of God.

Most people are not willing to pay the price to pick up their cross and follow Jesus. Matthew 16:24,25 (NIV) says, " ... If anyone would come after me, he must deny himself and take up his cross and follow me. For whoever wants to save his life will lose it, but whoever loses his life for me will find it." Many want to follow God but remain comfortable. This is not how it works. If you want to find out the truth in the Bible about how following Christ works, read the book of Matthew 10:17-42. You either follow Christ with everything in you, without compromise, or you serve two masters. And the Word says you cannot serve two masters in Matthew 6:24 (NIV), "No one can serve two masters. Either he will hate the one and love the other, or he will be devoted to the one and despise the other ...," The Word also says you should not be lukewarm either, or you will be spit out. Revelation 3:16 (NIV), "So, because you are lukewarm – neither hot nor cold – I am about to spit you out of my mouth." You are either on fire for God with all your mind, heart, body and soul – or you're as cold as ice with a solid and hardened heart before the Lord. Now I want to note that being on fire for God and serving Him with all your mind, heart, body and soul does not mean you will be perfect without making mistakes. This brings us to our main theme of repentance. The word tells us that a righteous man falls seven times, but gets back up again seven times. So long as you recognize your human limitations and inevitability of making mistakes, and correct them with true repentance and the infilling of the Holy Spirit, God can use you for His end time army.

There is hope for those who repent and turn around, because God is able and more than willing to fill you with wisdom and discernment, and He is fully capable of bringing you to where you need to be in Him, and where He wants you to be in this world – God communicates in many various ways according to His plan and purposes. Some receive dreams and visions; others hear the voice of God and know His voice (everyone is capable of this if God truly lives within you). To others He might give great signs, wonders and miracles. He might take you into His kingdom to have a conversation as He has done to some, or He may come to you and visit you physically and personally, as He has done to some others also. But whether big or small, God clearly communicates in ways that test us and build up our faith.

If we had little faith, how would we survive in the end times? You will be killed for following Christ in the end times, as they are already doing in some countries. God has a powerful message to reach out to all the souls of the Earth, and if we flee because of a small bit of persecution, then what are we? We are not the warriors God called us to be. Each trial and tribulation you face in your days is designed to build and strengthen your faith. Unanswered prayer is one of the greatest tools of building faith. How deeply is God embedded in your heart, that you will continue to petition and believe in Him for all your needs, even if they are unanswered for extended periods of time? How deep does your river of love run for God? Jesus taught about worrying, and in part of this explanation He said in Matthew 6:28-30 (NIV), "And why do you worry about clothes? See how the lilies of the field grow. They do not labor or spin. Yet I tell you that not even Solomon in all his splendor was dressed like one of these. If that is how God clothes the grass of the field, which is here today and tomorrow is thrown into the fire, will he not much more clothe you, O you of little faith?"

God wants us to have built up our most holy faith. You need faith to a high degree that you know you hear God's voice, and you listen to it and follow it to the completion of His will in your life. Look at Peter, who slipped in his faith as he denied Jesus three times. Jesus knew this already, but commanded Peter that once he repented and came back again, to strengthen his brothers and build up the church. And Peter did this faithfully, and because he learned from his mistakes, he was all the more strengthened and determined in his pursuit of bringing God's will here to Earth.

The assignments will keep coming; each one a test, each one with a purpose to fulfill. Every day of our lives, we will be beset by the enemy of our souls. He comes to buffet us, seeking to take us off course with all manner of tactics and deceptions. But God knows all, sees all and is everywhere. What better source of wisdom to defeat the enemy than from God Himself? It is the Spirit and power of God who abides in us that defeats the enemy. It is the abundance of the Holy Spirit inside of us that shines light into a darkened world. The level of light that shines through you in Christ is directly proportionate to how closely you are walking with God in truth and in spirit.

What we must understand is that the judgments that are coming upon this nation and all nations are nearly final judgments. Up until now, we have been slapped on the wrist and redirected with grace, mercy and long-suffering. People forget what life is like under God's anger or His wrath. It has happened before, just read the bible. People have become too comfortable in their sin, and as it was said before, they have mistaken God's patience for acceptance. What is happening is God is tired of simply “teaching lessons” with judgments and punishments and chastising. The days of Ananias and

Sapphira have returned, and this was spoken by God. The truth is people have lost their fear of God. They don't believe that in their complacency, anything bad could happen to them. These are the self-deceived. The judgments that are unfolding now are final judgments, tailored for the end times. Lesson learning time is over; it is time to use all you know of God's word to live your life and choose Heaven or Hell. Not one person is any higher than another. No one can work out your salvation for you. This is personal, it is real, and it is happening now. It is between you alone, and Almighty God. You must stand and face the Lord and answer Him as to what your decision is.

And I beheld a vision, as I was walking through the Earth there was darkness that came and fell across the land. Then there was a fog that was very thick and dense that rolled in on all sides. Lastly, there was a blizzard that came with heavy wet snow and fierce winds. The Lord revealed to me the interpretation of this dream – advanced darkness was coming into the land, gross darkness that covered the entire Earth. Even with a bright light of the gospel, the thick dense fog would scatter the light and cause confusion. Even with the voice of God to guide you and the obedience to His will, it would be difficult to move because of the extreme conditions of the blizzard.

It means that right now, today, we must have already been trained in God's full complete word. We must know how to perform spiritual warfare and take authority over the enemy in our lives, and we must already know God's voice and how to distinguish between the voices of God, the enemy, and the flesh. We must already be stable in obeying God's voice. We must already be battle hardened, if we are going to stand a chance in this coming storm that approaches the Earth because these are the end times and this is the beginning of the end.

Many people do not have the willingness to serve God completely, and many people do not have the faith required to step out and walk in God's will or even to hear His still small voice within. God is the Almighty one, and He is your Father that loves you unconditionally. Why do you doubt? Why do you believe He will not speak to you? Why do you look only to circumstances to find evidence of God? He abides within you, and He wants to talk to you and consume all of your senses. But your sin separates you from Him and the problems of communication are never on God's end – it is on your end every time.

Chapter 10: The End Times

I write this book as fulfillment of God's will for my life, and my only hope is that it will reach out to souls who hunger and thirst for something more – something they have tried to quench but could not. Something they have been searching this world for but could not find it. If you are one of these, who has this hunger and thirst for more in your life – something you feel you are missing that belongs with you, then look only to the Lord Jesus Christ. You need only look beside you, because He is truly with you even now to minister to you the hope and healing that comes from receiving His work on the cross. I pray that you will feel His peace wash over you to confirm that indeed you are worthy and indeed you are loved – so much so, that God gave His son to die and rise again as the atonement for your sins.

It is God, who desires that this book be written, and it is God who ministers and speaks through its pages, can you hear His still small voice calling out to you? He has been calling you since the moment you were born into this world, and He calls all of us until our last dying breath. But why wait until the end? It is a truly unique and fulfilling experience to willingly do His work.

In these last days, those who call themselves religious are no example at all. Religion has died, and only those who truly know Christ – and those who Christ in return also knows – will be able to make it through these seasons to come. A true follower of Christ will not come against man but rather the sin in a man, and those people, these children of God, will have compassion and love even to the unlovable. Rather than gossip or curse, they will seek diligent prayer and cast out the principalities within a person to set the captives free. A true child of God will live the same way in church that they do at home, and anywhere else they travel. A true child of God will be walking in the spirit and not the flesh – they will be ever ready to minister or prophesy or heal and pray in or out of season. They will know what takes place around them, as their eyes are open to the spirit realm and their ears are open to the voice of God as He leads guides and directs them.

What is the incentive to serve God if the enemy will attack you and cause you to suffer, seeking to bring you to the place where you give up on serving God? Because I myself have been in hell, and I saw many people with hopelessness written upon their faces, much sorrow and sadness that no human words could accurately define. Only through your eyes and your spirit could you understand the level of total hopelessness that exists. Weeping and mourning through everlasting torment, they beg only for Jesus to come and save them, but it is too late. Woe becomes them, and it is not worth giving up on

God during this temporary phase of existence, not when it has eternal consequences.

I am urging you all by the leading of the Holy Spirit, and I call you to repent. All sin has consequences, and many of you have been taught false doctrine and have been blinded by the enemy. Many leaders have led their flocks astray – and very few are making it in to the Kingdom. God weeps over the people in the end times, because very few are even ready or prepared. Perhaps God has been calling out, even crying out to you, because He wants you to be used and ready for His Kingdom. You must repent and open your hearts to the Holy Spirit. You must listen to the Holy One and not man, you must sincerely yield to God and allow Him to minister to you the TRUTH.

So many people have unique gifting and abilities given them by the Lord, and yet they have been twisted through deception and lies from the enemy to be used for worldly purposes to glorify themselves and have pride and haughtiness, even using their abilities for money and personal gain. These people are being manipulated by the prince of this world, and therefore God's desires are not being met by our choices. Yet when our desires are not met, the first one we place the blame on is God.

How do you think God feels? How frustrating is it when you know that you have everything figured out perfectly, and you know exactly how everything needs to play out for each person involved... yet when the project begins, everyone abandons all instruction and reason. Then they go off doing their own things and causing all manners of problems. Yet all the while, you're constantly crying out to them and giving them perfect instructions! But do they listen? No... they continue to believe you should not even be the project leader. After a while of this, you would be tempted to scrap the entire project. But God doesn't scrap you, and He doesn't give up on you either. And yes, you are definitely one who doesn't trust your project leader every time and goes off in your own direction. As humans that is our nature. But as spirit filled followers of Christ, our nature should be obedience, faith and love.

Maybe you have once served God and believed in the Word, yet somewhere down the line you changed your mind? I will tell you that we seldom change our minds in this area. What changes is our hearts, not our minds. The devil uses a situation, circumstance, thought or idea; and if you allow it, then it enters your mind gate where it has a chance to take root and grow into a foothold. As time passes and you entertain these thoughts rather than rebuking them and seeking God's wisdom and truth of the matter, they will continue to grow deeper roots and affect other areas of your thought life and belief system. Your faith is attacked, your obedience is attacked, your trust is attacked, etc.

Before you know it, this foothold becomes a stronghold. Now the enemy has a fortress installed in your temple and around your spirit, so that he can torment you and then hide in the place of darkness you have allowed growing within you. Most of us are not aware of the areas of spiritual darkness we have in us. Therefore we are not wise to the strategy the enemy is using against us, and we are blind to see when the enemy is actually attacking us – all the while he is deceiving us as he leads us away from Christ altogether. Check yourselves and your walk with God, even if you have fallen away, the Lord still calls you as He searches for His lost sheep. And once found, all of Heaven rejoices. (Read Matthew 18:12-14)

Chapter 11: The Death of the Flesh

I had always believed that my personality as it was would always be unchangeable. There was sin nature produced from my thought patterns and habits of mine that I believed were always just urges I had to live with. The world could not offer anything through learned words or texts, nor could the wisest person offer any wisdom or discernment that could teach me how to change some of the things buried at the core of my heart.

I have been in despair. That feeling when your life is falling apart and it feels like your marriage is about to break and all hell breaks loose. I know the feeling of being faced with the reality that your children might be taken away from you. I know what it feels like to lose your home, and be homeless with 6 children. I know the feeling of losing all your money and going without so your children can eat. It feels like a knife in your heart when your child looks disappointed at their portion of food, yet says nothing out of respect for you. It's one of those places that bring you quickly to your knees. I have cried out to God in these situations, but it has felt like He is not there. I have prayed but did not receive an answer. It is that feeling that you feel abandoned, that horrible feeling that God has left or forsaken you. I can tell you from personal experience that you will experience times like this in your walk with God, and it seems at times that God has left you. But I tell you the truth, God has never left you. The Almighty knows His children; and He knows what trials and persecutions will cause them to grow and learn.

The following is a prophetic Word from the Lord: “I do not desire that you will fall away from Me. I Am The Almighty One. Stick to Me and hold My hand. I am with you even in your darkest night and fiercest storm. When you do not feel Me, cast out all fear. I am within you. Hear My still small voice.”

My family has endured hell on all fronts; things so complicated that if I wrote about them this book would need to be labeled as science fiction in order for anyone to accept it. But my God is able, and He has never left us. The problem exists when we disobey God or step out of His will for our lives.

When we step ahead of God or lag behind Him, then we fall into valley’s that God never intended for us to go into. But the good news is that there is always a way out, for God has provided one. It takes earnest and sincere repentance and seeking God’s face about your issue. One of the hardest parts of walking out your calling with God is having fallen down and going through the valley of picking yourself back up while rebuking the guilt, shame and condemnation that comes with a fall. But the Word tells us in Proverbs 24:16 (NIV) “for though the righteous fall seven times, they rise again, but the wicked stumble when calamity strikes”. We are all human and will make mistakes, but the deeper we grow in Christ the more God expects of us to stay out of sin and die to our flesh.

I must stress the importance of obedience to God. The word 'disobedience' is not in God's vocabulary, according to what God told me one day. He speaks from obedience and cannot bless someone who is disobedient to Him. Sometimes the valley we are in lasts a lot longer than it should because we have failed to repent or realize that we have stepped out of God's Will for our lives. We must daily ask God to show us His heart. Only with a close and personal walk with Jesus Christ will we be able to have the Father's heart and eyes and ears to be able to walk through our lives in obedience to Christ.

Chapter 12: Spiritual Warfare

You do realize you are in the middle of a war zone, yes? Or did you think that Satan, the enemy of your soul, was going to freely let you return to God in Heaven without a fight? We must understand that this is not going to be easy, if you truly want to learn the deeper truths of God's Word. If you really desire to fulfill the calling God has upon your life by laying down your own will and leaning on His understanding and not your own – then you're in for the fight of your life. You will face circumstances designed to destroy you. You will face challenges that can rip apart your marriage or family. Matthew 10:34 (NIV) says, "Do not suppose that I have come to bring peace to the earth. I did not come to bring peace, but a sword." The word 'sword' in Greek is 'machaira' which is likely derived from 'mache' which means a battle or controversy (figuratively). Matthew 10:35 continues to explain how a man will come against his father, a daughter against her mother, and how a man's enemies will be the members of his own household. To follow Christ, you will be subject to much strife and suffering – yet you will have an eternal reward. This is what it means to pick up your cross and follow Him daily.

God warned me one time not to cast my pearls before the swine. I received this warning after

I had prayed for an issue in where I was disappointed and discouraged. I was recently born again and received all kinds of revelation about God and started walking in the gifts He ordained me to have, namely the seer and prophetic anointing's. I started to share this with someone close to me, out of excitement, I wanted them to share what I was feeling and receiving. Unbeknown to me, that person was not ready to hear what I had to say. Rightfully so, in their ignorance to the full Word, they were skeptical and started to cause me to doubt myself with some of their accusations. I started to let their words weigh me down and discourage me. That is when God told me not to cast my pearls before the swine. Matthew 7:6 (NIV) says, “"Do not give dogs what is sacred; do not throw your pearls to pigs. If you do, they may trample them under their feet, and turn and tear you to pieces.” This means it is futile to teach holy concepts to people who don’t want to listen and will only tear apart what we say. It is important to continue to teach unbelievers, but we must be discerning in what we say to whom so as not to waste our time.

The enemy, the devil, will operate through anyone who has an open door in their lives to allow him in. In spiritual warfare you must understand we are not fighting other people. The best reference is Ephesians 6:12 (NIV) “For our struggle is not against flesh and blood, but against the rulers, against the authorities, against the powers of this dark world and against the spiritual forces of evil in the heavenly realms."

When people are hateful towards us, there are a multitude of things happening behind the scenes that we do not see with our fleshly eyes. Some form of event or trauma has taken place in their lives which has not yet been healed. Bitterness has taken root in their hearts, or possibly they have become unforgiving. That has opened a door for the enemy to come inside and use their thoughts, emotions, and personality to come against people. There is a spirit of anger or bitterness or any other type that could be operating through that person. Demons are trespassers; they sometimes invade your house unwanted. But if you don't do anything about it, do they have to leave? No. If someone stands on your property, trespassing, and you do nothing about it – they will make a tent and camp on your land. That tent, if left unchecked, starts getting bigger as more people flock to it. After all, it's okay. It is better to tell the one person to leave your property and use your authority and power to cast them off your land, rather than to face a multitude that can resist you.

Notice I said use your power *and* authority. Of course, this is Christ's power and authority. We have none of our own, and if we try to use our own, the devil and his demons will laugh at us and destroy us. Using what Christ gave us, we are victorious; but only if we understand what we were given and only if we know how to use it.

The enemy knows the calling on our lives; he knows how much God has anointed us and just how powerful God has made us in Him. But he lies to us as part of his attacks, convincing us that we are unworthy and not good enough to be used by God. But only when you truly understand God's nature, God's love, and God's forgiveness can you begin to see the pure Grace that has made us worthy in Christ Jesus. The devil doesn't want you to know the simple truth that you have all power and authority to trample over him and his demons. Satan wants to trick you into thinking there are some things he's just too powerful for you to do anything about. It is true that Satan is a supernatural being with much power, and if we faced him head on with our own strength we would surely stumble and fall. So we must have Jesus Christ living in us, and we must be obedient to God and striving to live Holy lives, keeping true repentance in our hearts with a righteous fear of God. If we follow these principles and standards of Holy living, the devil can never kill us or take us under.

The Word of God is a weapon, a sword. This is your tool to attack the enemy. And yes, you must take the offensive while keeping your defense up. Jesus resisted Satan in the desert, and note that He used the Word of God every time. The devil cannot stand against the Word of God. He knows its power; he knows it is the truth that cannot be refuted. James 4:7 (NIV) says, “Submit yourselves, then, to God. Resist the devil, and he will flee from you.” Note here it says first that you must submit to God. Without this critical step, you’re already defeated. Then you must resist the devil as Jesus did. When you face temptations or problems, speak to the powers and principalities in heavenly realms and quote the Word of God. Remember, you’re not fighting other people – but the darkness that influences them.

Chapter 13: The Church

This is a hard truth many might not accept – but God has said that He is done with the church. Many have been sitting in the house of God, sitting under the anointing and learning the deeper truths of the Word. Yet these people have not changed. I have personally witnessed people sit under a powerful anointing and learn about as deep a truth as I have ever seen, yet they prefer their sin nature and refuse God's grace and they do not repent. I see many others who are equipped to know better, yet they are totally self-deceived. God is getting ready to make a powerful move like the church has never seen before. Religion is dead and out the window, God is now using those who have yielded to Him and are obedient to Him. God is now shifting all His focus into the world. God will use the prostitutes, the drug addicts, and the worst of the worse. He will bring them in and clean them up; then use them mightily. God has expressed anger and disappointment at the church, because the church should know better and has no excuse. He has called and called, and visited and visited, but the body as a whole still cannot get it together. Only the small remnant will be allowed to participate in God's great glory drop.

We are about on the cutting edge of what God is doing for this end time hour. It is so critical and important that we stay focused on God and nothing else. There is too much deception going on in the world, and if you are not solid and stable knowing who you are in Christ then you will truly be swallowed up by the gross darkness that is about to fall upon America.

There is a great deception falling over the nation, a great veil that will shadow the eyes of truth. The Word tells us that if possible, even the elect will be deceived (Matthew 24:24 NIV). There is coming a time where people who claim to follow God will lure you into traps to have you killed. There is coming a time where the world system, ruled by Satan from the heavenly realms of evil, will seek to destroy all that profess Christ. There will be a tightly knit together system in which everything is monitored and surveyed, all data and information that could be collected – will be collected. All this data will be transferred to centers where it is filtered and analyzed. The devil will use any means necessary to be "like God". Because he loves to counterfeit God, he will design and institute a world system of control to mimic the Omni-presence of God.

Everything that is said or done, even what we do behind closed doors (or so we believe) can and will be made known to the enemy. This is not done by a supernatural power of Omniscience, because Satan is a limited and a created being, but rather by the influence he has on the world system and technology to be used for dark purposes. You will be astonished at how the devil has overtaken technology, to the degree that in the days he reigns over the Earth, a simple Christian conversation in your living room, or the mention of the word "Jesus" over the telephone or E-Mail, is enough to have the one-world military force to execute you for not following the one-world religion which serves the Anti-Christ.

The bible tells us that the mark of the beast is required to buy, sell, or trade. Even so, that all shall be bound to it, both small and great, rich and poor, free and bond. This implies that there is a system in place that can monitor the human population, which has mankind registered in a central database system. A law will be decreed that all who do not worship the beast shall be killed. Because this is not a law created by the simple imagination of mankind; therefore lackadaisical in its enforcement, in contrast to a law created by the will and authority of a supernatural being with the greatest magnitude of evil, such a law would be supernaturally enforced with extreme vigor.

It would then seem to appear as though the depth and severity of a governmental system ruled by the supernatural influence of Satan, even then physically manifested on the Earth, having been given authority and power over it for a time, would create an environment of extreme persecution for true Christians who profess Christ unto death. Yet because our God is greater than our adversary, and greater than all things, we have power and authority to overcome the devil and his hosts even in the face of this revelation.

God will equip those He calls, and we must look to Isaiah 59:19 in these end times because when the enemy comes in with full assault force, God will raise a standard against him. God's grace is truly sufficient.

You will also see a lot of churches being established in people's homes in this end time hour, as many of the world's churches and mega-ministries will fall under the oppression, especially as God is lifting His grace from the church scene and is transitioning to those who will hear His call in the world.

Chapter 14: The Legal System

In our world we have a legal system that is established to create and uphold law and order. It is intended to be fair and balanced, but in our imperfect world it doesn't always work out to be that way. There are law abiding citizens and there are criminals who violate the laws, and a multitude in between. When someone has a dispute, the issue is taken first to law enforcement. Charges against parties take place at this time and a hearing is made in court as those involved stand before a judge. The judge reviews evidence and assesses the charges, and has authority to declare the law and to punish according to the law. Once a sentence is carried out, the judgment is enforced.

This same principle applies in the spirit realm. The main difference is that God's system is perfect, righteous, just, and holy. Sometimes demons can't be cast out of people right away; not because of lack of power and authority but because of legal rights that spirits obtain. We must be discerning and have wisdom from God when dealing with people that are oppressed or possessed with demons. The enemy goes before God and gets permission first before he can do anything. We see this fact in the book of Job. The spirit realm is filled with such a mind boggling legal system. God even allows those who don't serve Him to come against those who do. There are some forms of oppression and torment that will not go away no matter how much praying is done; because that request may not be in God's will. These thorns in your flesh have a purpose to them, just look at when Paul was in prison. He asked God three times to remove the thorn from his flesh but God only replied that His grace was sufficient for Paul. Then one day that thorn was suddenly removed. But the key to that was Paul praised God even in the midst of his suffering...

In spiritual warfare, we can evict the enemy from the premises that he has no legal right to inhabit. Think of this analogy: you inherit a piece of land and build a house. Your property is beautiful and spacious; it is delightful because it is yours. This is how God created our vessels to be. Now along comes a vagrant, a lawless person who says to himself, “This house looks well to do, and I could profit from in habiting its territory. I will first go to its border and patrol it, to test the boundary. (This is what happens as we experience temptations). As we yield and compromise to temptation, we invite sin. The vagrant then steps onto our property and says to himself, “I have trespassed and yet I am still here, I will take advantage of this master's possessions and his land, his home, and all that is in it. First I will camp beside his home in a tent.” The vagrant has now established a foothold, and as you neglect to participate in spiritual warfare, the studying and application of God's word, and the oneness with you and God, that vagrant invites his wicked friends to join him. Now the vagrant and his allies build houses on your property, because until now you have not enforced your power and authority to remove them from your land. It has now become a stronghold, and it is much more difficult to remove and evict someone who is deeply rooted and grounded upon your land. They are not willing to leave after building large homes to operate from, and communities to exchange power and ability. (These are demons and groupings of demons that your active sin has allowed to thrive within you).

You were equipped with power and authority from the beginning, and if you had used it knowing who you are in Christ, the vagrant would have never crossed your border in the first place.

The enemy is very cunning and deceiving and his greatest trick is convincing people that they are powerless and have no authority over him and his kingdom. The people need to understand that they do have power and authority over the enemy, the bible tells us this fact. Do you have the faith to walk it out and believe it?

When you use Christ's authority to rebuke the enemy, he doesn't go running in the opposite direction until he's out of sight. A strong rebuke will cause him to take one step back – he is testing you to see if you really believe in the authority you appear to use. He takes another step back and tries to lie and deceive you with circumstances to trick you into believing it didn't work. Will you give in to it so he can take two steps forward to torment you? Or will you remain solid and firm and continue to use your authority over him, causing him to flee?

The devil knows whether you really mean something or not, so be wise and do not become proud or arrogant. Stay humble before the Lord and be submissive to God, so that He can use you mightily and you will stand before the enemy on solid ground.

We must realize that we can do nothing on our own without God. When we face supernatural powers that could easily consume us, we must recognize our own weakness and inferiority. There should be nothing in you that resents the truth of this weakness, nothing in you that resists being powerless of your own strength, for it is Christ Jesus who strengthens you *in* your weakness. When we learn to submit to the Lord and allow Him to operate fully and completely through us, the spirit realm is flooded with God's power and all manner of strongholds and demonic powers and principalities are destroyed.

Many times we cannot see the manifestations in the physical realm of God's work, and it appears as though nothing is happening or that God is not working on our behalf, and sometimes it feels like our prayers have not been answered or that God has left us. But I tell you from personal experience, everything happens in the spiritual realm first. The warring that takes place on our behalf is spiritual and takes place in a realm we cannot see or feel with our senses. We must be close to God to be able to see in the spirit realm, and then He can show us all that is being done on our behalf.

God wants us to praise and worship Him and also give Him thanks for all that He is doing in our lives. It would stand to reason that God is willing to show you all He's doing for you and on your behalf, for the purpose of allowing you to praise and worship Him for all that He is doing!

There is power and breakthrough in praise and worship! You have not yet seen the wonders of Heaven, the glorious presence of Almighty God, you have not yet even touched the surface of the heart of God! Genuine praise and worship is the key to your breakthrough. The enemy hates the saints praising and worshiping God, he knows its power and its effects. I praise God that He supernaturally delivered me from alcohol, drugs, pills, and a life of destruction. The power of God is greater than anything and when you experience it, it will forever change you. Because of the redemptive power of Jesus Christ and what He did for you on the cross, you have the right to stand before God in the court room of Heaven and plead your case (Hebrews 7:25 NIV).

In your intercessory prayer, you may boldly approach the Throne of Grace and petition God to hear your case. It is best to ensure alone time with God and accurately hear the voice of God, and first pray for the Holy Spirit to pray with you and decree that the enemy shall not bind or hinder your prayers and that they will go directly to the Throne of Grace immediately. At this, ask for the assistance of the angelic host to elevate you into the third heavens, a realm higher than "... the rulers, ... the authorities, ... the powers of this dark world and ... the spiritual forces of evil in the heavenly realms." (Ephesians 6:12 NIV)

Now pray and ask for The Lord Jesus Christ to intercede for you, to intermediate for you on your behalf. It is now the time to allow the Holy Spirit to pour itself out on you and make your case, and allow God time to deliberate and consider your case. Come prepared, for the enemy is always present in this place. He is the accuser of the brethren, and any time you go into the court room of The Most High, he will also be there with his case prepared to destroy your image and reputation if you step out in the flesh.

If you keep your focus in the Spirit, recognizing that it is only by Christ Himself that you have any power or right, the devil cannot put a black mark on you. However, if you claim any right or boast of any feat, any accomplishment or make any assumption towards God, the enemy will defeat you with the written law. You must keep your focus on Jesus Christ as your source and authority; for He came not to abolish the law, but to fulfill it. Be careful what you say in the court room, as even here there are angelic stenographers that record every word you speak. With Christ, the enemy cannot use the written law against you. Christ never violated the law, He is pure and blameless.

God will honor any request you make in the court room, if it lines up with His will, by rooting and grounding yourself in Jesus Christ as your only source. The enemy would love to see us step out of God's will, and into our own fleshly understanding and false power. It is here that he strikes and knocks us down because we are walking on shifting sands.

The will of God for your life is to bring you good, to prosper you. Yes, you will suffer. The bible tells us this plainly. You must realize that as you follow Jesus, He will dwell inside you more and more as you become obedient and deeper with Him. As this occurs, the darkness in the people of the world and around you will come against the Light of Christ in you. You will see this manifest itself through people's actions, behavior, and even in the spirit realm through dreams and visions and other gifting's God can use to warn us.

God is Holy and just, righteous in everything He does. We must come to understand that there is a legal system in place and while God is sovereign and in control of all things, He does follow His own legal system. It may dishearten Him greatly to have to allow you to go through a valley, and it may be the very last thing He desires for you to go through... but because of your own free will, and the legality the enemy works with, God will allow it.

I have heard God speak over people weeping and crying, wailing over them. Saying to them that He never intended for this to happen, He never wanted them to go through this... but He must allow it, because of the choices they made. This is because it is a consequence of disobedience. This kind of thing can be avoided and even to some extent reversed by repenting and trusting God with your future and life and becoming totally obedient.

www.ingramcontent.com/pod-product-compliance
Lightning Source LLC
Chambersburg PA
CBHW060510030426
42337CB00015B/1838

* 9 7 8 0 9 9 7 4 5 4 1 1 6 *